PURPOSE DOESN'T CARE WHAT'S IN YOUR BANK ACCOUNT

PROTECTING YOUR MENTAL HEALTH IN BUSINESS THROUGH FAITH

Jeff, I know that the journey can feel cloudy at times but I hope this book helps you remember that the sun, that HOPE lives within you!

— Sabriya Dobbins

By Sabriya Dobbins
Founder of Project Passport

Purpose Doesn't Care What's in Your Bank Account:
Protecting Your Mental Health in Business Through Faith

First printing April 2022

For more information, contact:

Sabriya Dobbins
4058 13th Street #1044
St. Cloud, FL 34769

Scripture quotations are taken from The Holy Bible: New International Version and English Standard Version.

Cover design: Leanna Van Der Have
Interior design: Leanna Van Der Have
Editor: Lynn Hall

ISBN: 978-0-578-36582-4

Printed in America.

www.sabriyadobbins.com

DEDICATION

I dedicate this book to all of the unheard hearts and souls trying to make it on the journey. I know you feel alone. I know you are scared. Allow this book to become your blanket to shelter you from the storm.

TABLE OF CONTENTS

INTRODUCTION

Before you get into this book, let me be upfront with you. I'm no pastor. I am not a biblical expert, and I am surely not a perfect Christian. While I try every day to be better than I was the day before, I still get this thing called life wrong over and over. I do not know a ton of Bible verses off the top of my head, nor do I know the Lord's prayer fully. To be honest, I don't even go to church every Sunday. At one point in my life, I did not even think I was worthy of God's love, and I surely did not love myself. It took rock bottom, loss, despair, and wanting to give up on my life before I got to this positive, peaceful space.

Despite the chaotic moments of my life, I know one thing is for sure. I did not write this book by happenstance, and you are not reading it by accident. This book is a message God sent me to deliver from my life to yours. He did not ask me to write you a flawless story with sunshine and rainbows. Instead, He instructed me to follow Him and to inspire entrepreneurs like you to see *who* they were created to be, along with *what* they are meant to create. Right now, you may be considering a new business or non-profit, and you want to ensure God is a part of the foundation somehow. Or you may already be standing at the helm of your business at this moment, and you realize that you are missing a key team player and a bomb business coach, God. Either way, you are now armed with the right resource by making the decision to pull this book from the shelf, to read it, and to act on what you learn.

I have some even better news. You do not have to be the perfect Christian to benefit from this book. God knows that you will and have made mistakes as we all do. Lord knows I have. I will probably make more tomorrow and the next day as you will too. Nonetheless, He loves you for your willingness to turn to Him to become a better version of yourself—the version He created you to be. He loves you for allowing Him to help you live out the beautiful purpose He has carefully designed for you. You may not talk to God often or you may not know Him well at all. Fortunately, He knows you really well and He is waiting for you to simply open the door to pick up wherever you left off or to start anew. There is no judgement, only love in this place. And I promise you, this book will mirror God's heart of love, guidance, and compassion for you. Now, I did not promise there wouldn't be any tough love because there will be but I will be there every step of the way. We are in this together now and God is the guiding light for us both.

The number one lesson I have learned throughout my entire life's journey is that I am not at a beauty pageant for the world to get some version of Sabriya they believe I should be. This is real life. The biggest goal of this journey is to show Him through me. In all the work that I do and in all of the projects I take on, if I cannot represent the light God shines through me, then it is not the right project for me. When I started my business, I did not have much money nor business skills. I thought I was out of my mind to really believe it would work, and now I have changed the lives of hundreds, if not thousands, of people through my company. Furthermore, I thought I was crazy to write this book in just a few months. Many people take years to write, but God poured everything I needed to share with you at the tip of my fingers. Thousands of words later, it graces your hands, and it is right where it needs to be. I made something out of nothing with God on my side.

Something out of nothing… this remains the theme of my life. With God, I am constantly creating something extraordinary starting with the ordinary.

God did not ask you to have it all figured out before you begin your business. He made one a simple request: For you to follow Him and trust Him, especially when you cannot see the way ahead. I like to compare your path of faith to a Michael Jackson music video. It's the one where every step he took, the floor lit up, perhaps reminding him he was exactly where he was supposed to be. That is how your path with God works. You may not know which step to take in your life and business, but when you are willing to take steps, God is willing to help illuminate the path that you cannot see.

The best part about this whole book is that even through the hard parts we will go through together, know that the end will be joyous. This is not about your past. It doesn't matter what you have done or what you have said. It doesn't matter who you were. What matters most is who you are becoming, which is the person you are meant to be. From this moment on, I want you to focus on using the phrase (as a mentor once told me): *"from now on."* What happened then was then; what is happening now is between **Team You and God**.

With God on your team and you as the entrepreneur, world changer, inspiration creator, the odds are forever tilted in your favor. You will be successful spiritually, emotionally, financially, and in every way possible. You will find peace. You will find hope. There is no other alternative. You are on a winning team! Now it is time to start acting like it.

PART I: IN THE BEGINNING

Just as the world has a creation story,
your business does too.

CHAPTER 0.5:
HOW TO READ THIS BOOK

You know the best part about writing your own book? You get to make up chapter numbers! Yes, I am that difficult person that always has to make my own rules. So I broke the book rules and made up a partial chapter title. I really do believe this is more of a partial chapter, hence I named it "Chapter 0.5." It did not need a whole one! I feel really good about myself right about now. Okay, enough of feeling myself. What is the point of this chapter? I want to make sure you understand how to read this book.

Throughout your read, you will notice that sometimes I enter a chapter with a portion labeled "Storytime" or sometimes I just talk directly to you, imparting my best attempt at wisdom. Just minus all of the fancy words and eloquent quotes because I am just a girl who lives in leggings and tees. I am no ball gown wearing, wine loving princess. I am so awkward and silly no matter how hard I try haha so bear with me. See, there I go on my soapbox. By the way, expect some mini tangents throughout this book. It is who I am as a person and this would not be a real book if you did not get to see the real me in action. And that means losing my train of thought with plenty of tangents that are so very relevant in a weird, funny kind of way. See now let me bring you back to where we were.

Bottom line, I just want you to get what you need from this book and to get it quickly. I try to be straightforward with my advice and as clear as possible with my stories. Either way, each time I go into my stories, you will have the indication that the imaginary campfire is appearing when you see the word "Storytime" as I am about to share real facts about my life's experiences. Try to imagine yourself there with me or reflect on what you have experienced similarly as you read. When you see the squiggle (‿ℓℓℓ‿), this means I am transitioning back into a conversation directly to you with the meaty lessons to share from my experiences.

At the end of each chapter, I provide life application activities and discussion for you to complete. I am really big about tangible tools so you can start making changes immediately. You are going to want to have access to a journal in order to follow along. At the end... end, end of the chapters, I provide take away tips and quotes for you to use how you see fit. I say print the ones you love most and stick them on your walls to keep you grounded.

This book is not a read-once-and-then-never-open-it-up-again kind of book. It is one to reference time and time again as you face life's challenges. You'll think: "Dang X is happening to me. Let me find that chapter she wrote on this topic." Well at least that is my goal for you. Enough of the logistics. I think you are ready. Are you ready? Not sure? Well, it's too late. You are here! Might as well stay. You are too invested now.

So... as I promised, this is Chapter 0.5 because it's short and sweet. Just to get you started. Now jump into the car (our imaginary one). Let's go for a ride, maybe hit a few curbs or two. But did you die? Well, we will see!

CHAPTER 1:
IT IS NOT WHAT YOU THINK

STORYTIME

I remember sitting in my prayer closet (aka my actual closet stuffed with way too many clothes) weeping with tears and a stuffy nose. So, wow I came out of the gate rhyming and that was not even the plan. Haha, wait no tangents already! Back to my story...

I could barely breathe, taking sharp breaths in between every overwhelming burst of emotion that left my eyes and body. What in heck was I going to do? Everything felt completely out of my reach and control. The news that I was just watching flash across the screen painted a picture of chaos. It painted a grim picture of the year to come, and the sad part was that we were only in March 2020. It was like the world took its hand and gave everyone the slap in the face of their lives. Little did I know, there were years of chaos to come. Not to mention, in the months before, my family experienced a severe psychotic break situation with my younger brother, and as the "mental health person" of the family, I had to navigate it all. After the ordeal had ended, we finally thought we were going to be able to breathe and finish out the year of 2020 in peace. If you are a human on this earth, aware of the pandemic, you know just how wrong we were to think this was going to end so easily.

But nope. A freaking pandemic single-handedly knocked Project Passport, my precious company, to the ground, and I was still reeling from the mental health crisis that had stricken my family. People were sick and dying, businesses falling apart, the world was just a mess. I did not know what to think. The nauseous feeling in my stomach made me want to run to the bathroom and never leave. *Why would God help me get my first clients just to take them away? How could He bring me this far, a little over a year in business, just to leave me?* All my thoughts were slapping my brain like a ton of bricks. I felt like the stupidest entrepreneur and a failed leader.

How could I have not prepared for a pandemic? Yeah, I should have had everything figured out because, as an entrepreneur, I have control over my life and career. I should have been prepared for the worst, right? The months were grueling with refund after refund being processed out of money we simply did not have as a company. The money had already been spent on a retreat we were determined to go on in July 2020. I remember saying over and over that this retreat to Kenya had to happen because it was the opening pinnacle of what Project Passport had to offer. It had to happen. This was our first retreat, and after months of struggling to get people to even book with us, nothing was going to stop my team and I. NOTHING. It was like the universe said: *Oh really? Nothing huh? How about a great big pandemic?*

It is funny how the stages of grief just burst into your home without even knocking. Despair, anger, denial, bargaining, and acceptance alternated as themes of my days. While I wallowed in my pity party for weeks, I felt even more guilt and frustration because I knew people were suffering worse than me, yet I was still bawling my eyes out. So much time and money had been placed into the loving hands of 2020, and in one fell swoop, it was all gone. I knew I was not alone, but somehow, the experience felt more isolating than I could ever imagine. The walls were closing in, and my strength was wavering like a leaf in the wind. Control—I just felt like I had lost control. I had everything else that entrepreneurs were supposed to have. You know that stuff we call ambition, leadership, and charisma? Wasn't that enough? But then again, the real question was: *Did I ever have any control in the first place?*

ele

I think I might have read more than fifty books on entrepreneurship, hundreds of blogs, listened to tons of podcasts, and have probably watched one too many YouTube videos. This is especially true as a new entrepreneur. I had a desperate need to do things right. I wanted to look the part, act the part, speak the part, and if possible, even smell the part. It is hilarious how entrepreneurship is depicted as some journey of freedom, unicorns, and me, me, me, and yet, that is not how it works.

Another thing I always hear from some entrepreneurs when they are asked what made them so successful: *It took passion. It took grit. It took dedication. It took perseverance. It took commitment.* While all of those are great things that help concoct the recipe of "success," I think that many of them are falling short on a key ingredient. Rarely do I hear them say what I choose to tell people: **"It takes: Raw. Blind. Faith."** Not just some faith in yourself or faith in the universe, which both help, but true faith in knowing that God, the Divine, has His hand directly on your path.

To be clear, I am not talking about those quick acceptance speeches that athletes and movie stars give at ceremonies where they throw a quick shout-out to God and that is that. It is wild faith. I am talking about what Joyce Meyer said: "Remember that the same power that raised Jesus from the dead is within you." I am talking about that faith that scientists may call irrational, yet I call miracles. Now, do not get overwhelmed when I say this because no matter where you are in the journey, you can achieve wild faith. Grit, perseverance, and passion combined cannot cradle you, inspire you, teach you, protect you, and care for you like the power of faith in God. You need the faith to direct all of the helpful entrepreneurship qualities that you carry. When the pandemic hit, I had all of those "good business owner" qualities, but they meant nothing if I did not have strong faith.

Entrepreneurship can give you the illusion of freedom and control, however, it is one of the things you have the least amount of control over because it depends on other human beings. You cannot control other human beings, and often, you have to adjust your path to fit their needs in business. In addition, it is not about what you can get. It is about how you can best serve the population you are here to help. It is about what you can do to make their lives better. That is what the experience is truly about if you want to find success that is emotionally, mentally, and financially immense.

The only control you have over this entire process is how you react to the process. I react by leaning on faith and not carrying the burdens of what I cannot control in my own heart. Now, I did not immediately do this during my pity party, but I did find my way back.

You cannot do anything as long as you are focused on what you cannot do.

Now, I want you to stop for a second and ask yourself some honest questions. Are you waking up at 3:00 a.m. every day hitting the pavement hard and not getting the results you want? Are you losing client deal after client deal, and you do not understand why? Are you cringing over those negative reviews you just received? They always say, when it rains, it pours but I need you to understand that maybe you are so busy trying to run from the rain instead of redirecting the rain to water the right plants in order for you to get the harvest you are dreaming of.

Okay, now I am speaking in all of these weird philosophical quotes... probably throwing you off. The bottom line is that you need to let faith become the forefront of all of those things you are experiencing. Yes, you need to be disciplined, but you need faith for when you are not seeing those "discipline results" you are looking for. Yes, you are going to lose client deals, but you must have enough faith to understand they were not your clients to receive at the moment. It sucks to get a crappy review, but you must have faith you will use the right feedback and trash the advice that does not make sense for your business. You have to have faith that a pandemic won't take you and your business out, even when things look bad. Stop trying to carry everything on your shoulders all on your own. You are a human being with human emotions. The spiritual space that you belong to houses miracles, breakthroughs, and perfect right-place-right-time moments. It does not depend on human power but a fuel source that trumps all of humanity, the desire of God for you to succeed.

STORYTIME

Things were beginning to normalize in the best way they could for me. Thankfully, I had received some government assistance to fill in the financial gaps. While we were still in the midst of the storm, I began to feel a sense of calm wash over me. The time in my prayer closet was not about the present or the past but what I could create for the future. The ideas came to me in sparks. Maybe, just maybe... I can... do this.

As a company, we began to host virtual mental wellness retreats for women, and we received raving reviews filled with joy. I remember one woman saying that one of our purpose retreats created a breakthrough moment within her that she could have never expected. Another attendee shared that she now understood what was important to her because of the retreat with us. While we could not take these women around the world to change their lives, we were doing it from behind a computer screen! We had created a new arena of virtual retreating! We were changing the game. We hosted a huge virtual mental health event with the National Alliance of Mental Health (NAMI) of Durham. We were breaking the barriers of access to mental wellbeing before our very eyes. We were on to something, and it was even bigger than the original plan we had less than a year ago.

What had changed? Why was this working? Why was my life getting better, even though it seemed like the world was not?

I knew in my heart it had everything to do with my lens. My faith lens was firmly in place, and I remembered that this pandemic was happening to everyone, not just me. God did not single out Project Passport to take us out. Darkness wanted to throw the world a dirty curveball and God was dusting away the rubble so I could see the road ahead. My prayers were no longer about fixing what was broken with Project Passport, as they were about divine and unique ideas that would change the world in which we now lived in. I had to rev up the fuel source of faith that would guide me into a very successful year two of business in the mid- to final quarter of 2020.

The greatest gift of it all was realizing my company was so much more than a travel retreat. We had something special at our core that transcended virtual, travel, and everything in between. It was our interactive, hands-on mental wellbeing products that truly changed lives and evolved futures. Our content, delivery, and compassion were what the world needed. Nothing more, nothing less. The crutch of travel in which I had been leaning on was moot. We had a unique concept, and it stood the test of external impacts, even a pandemic. We were just that good. Nonetheless, I acknowledged there was nothing I could do about the external circumstances of my situation, and I learned that sheer blind faith and a heart willing to listen was all I needed to navigate the figurative, and in some cases, literal hurricanes that I was facing along with the rest of the world. Faith allowed me to perfectly place my charisma, perseverance, drive, and innovation where it needed to be. My team, with God in the front, became unstoppable.

WHAT DOES THIS MEAN FOR YOU?

Okay, so you read about my peril and maybe it mirrored yours, and maybe it did not. The point is, everything you need to make this business journey a success starts with one key choice: FAITH. If you decide to add faith to your equation, it will always check out. Had I decided to fix the mess on my own, I would have succumbed to the pressure. There are one too many stories of entrepreneurs experiencing nervous breakdowns, committing suicide, and experiencing extreme unhappiness in the face of unexpected obstacles. I think about the CEO, Tony Hsieh, who tragically died in a fire back in 2020. He struggled with severe mental issues causing him to act out recklessly and many people were his enablers. I read about another CEO who started a marketing and devOps company but after living the path of sheer burnout and chaos, he had a severe mental breakdown, and he did not even know who he was. He spent days recovering in the hospital, but he was never the same again. Kate Spade, Kent Taylor, and the list goes on of CEOs who have taken their lives, under the crushing pressure of the world. After they have lost control and went through these failures, they just cannot withstand or carry them alone. Some things are not made for man (or woman, in my case) to handle alone. Most things are not within our control, no matter how much we believe they are.

For example, you may have the most magnificent event planned in the world that must be an outdoor experience. In your head, there is no other way. No matter what you say or do, you will have absolutely no control over if the weather decides to deteriorate and drench the space where your event sits. Your faith says: "No matter what happens outside of your control, divine support and guidance, will help you make the next best move." Whether you change the event location or move the event online, postpone the event, or do something even more creative, your faith is the control mechanism, and you are just seeing the outcome through.

I want you to do a self-check and ask yourself these questions (go ahead and jot down your answers too):

- What have you been using as the primary fuel to your business? Ex: Do you have plenty of cash to make it run? Do you have the "perfect" innovative eye?

- What would happen if you switched your main fuel source to faith? Do you feel it would hurt or help your business and how so?

- What does pure, blind faith mean to you? Is it reckless? Why or why not?

Honestly, there are no right answers to these questions. Let's just say, there are better case scenario outcomes if you select certain responses. I cannot force you to choose faith as your fuel, as you may find success with other fuel sources. However, in total transparency, my faith was built to last through the storm. My engine will not die, and there is an endless supply of my faith fuel, even if I forget to use it from time to time. Faith just does not run out. You may find it elusive at times, but you can always access it again and again.

God + Business Tip #1: Set faith upfront as a

foundational aspect of your business model. It will save you from a world of hurt in the long run!

(And do not worry as we will talk about how to keep your faith flag steady throughout the rest of the book!)

Save this quote to keep you going:

"Unlike money, faith never runs out in business. It is the one asset that does not depreciate, and it is your most lucrative operations budget to work with."

CHAPTER 2:
THE SILENCE HAS A VOICE

Something peculiar happens when you spend time in that silent space you discover within the world. Everyone is not always as lucky to find the silence, however when they find the rare gem, it elicits a ripple effect of change. If you attended traditional school, you could relate to this. Ever since we were children, we grew up believing the silence was important for two reasons: 1) Learning in school and 2) To stay out of trouble when asked to be quiet. The silence was almost forced upon us, although some children are naturally more silent than others. I was one of those kids on the opposite end of the spectrum. I remember the constant notes of talking on all of my report cards by teachers. "She is very intelligent, but she is talking in class often." But I was done with my work and had nothing better to do! What did these teachers expect? I was bored! Funny thing is, everything I do now is truly based on my talent in speaking. I literally get paid to talk; go figure.

Nonetheless, I learned a really important lesson about silence early on in my entrepreneurship journey. Silence is actually a necessity. Have you ever heard someone say, they heard the booming, powerful voice of God? I am sure you have read one of the stories or perhaps watched a television episode about a person's experience. Honestly, I would probably freak out if I did! While I have never heard the in-room, in your ear, booming voice of God, I have had words and messages from Him etched into my heart at times, and in some instances, I even get it on paper.

I think many people who pray create this one-way conversation with God filled with requests and statements. There rarely is room for God to truly respond. We can be so worried about saying everything we have to say. We pray, get up, and go distract ourselves with another part of life. We don't even wait and listen for an answer! Life is like the sound that televisions used to make when you turned the cable box off, and the screen had the grey static picture on it with the loud scratchy sound. I remember if my volume was too high at night, it would scare the mess out of me, and I would about jump out of my clothes. As I grew older, I realized that much of my life began to feel just like the television screen: static, voices, words, thoughts.

Truth be told, there was no peace and no silence.

Whether you are looking to start a business or if you currently run a business, you need the ideas and innovation to help you thrive. To put all the pressure on yourself to figure it all out is a disservice to your happiness. The number one lifeline that answers every single call is God, but you must be willing to pick up the phone. The silent line has a voice, and it is a voice that speaks directly to your heart. You have got God 911 and 1-800-God, all on speed dial. Pick up the phone!

ele

STORYTIME

"I made a huge mistake. This is not going to work."
I remember uttering those embarrassing words over

the phone to my significant other, Taylor. I could not believe I had just dropped my entire real estate career that I hated, just to move into another job that I was already unhappy with. It was September 2018 and it was day two at my new job in higher ed, and I knew I had messed up. The people were great, and the work was easy. Yet, this was the exact problem! It was just too simple. I was trying to be this perfectly polished working professional who had graduated college, but I honestly looked more like a little kid trying to wear their mom's clothing that was too big, and I looked as silly as could be. Clobbering around in her oversized high heels trying to feel like someone who knew what was going on in life. I was lost. How in the heck did I finish college recently just to end up like this? I just could not understand why I was not happy with my decent paycheck and my peaceful little job.

When the opportunity to move to Belize with Taylor for a few months arose later that same year, I was relieved to escape my unhappiness, although I was just as terrified because I had no game plan. I would leave this job and then what? Taylor had gotten a position working as an Information Technologist for an overseas contract, and they wanted him there as soon as possible. He had to do a bit of urging on my end because part of me was tempted to stay in my role for the sake of comfort. What would I do living in Belize with no job? At the time, the idea of some inspirational life discovery experience through travel was floating around my head. I did not have much lined up, even though I tried to appear confident when I told my managers I was leaving to pursue my own endeavors. I had only been working at the job for about four or five months before I was whisked away by an airplane with my bags in tow to live overseas until... whenever.

Some blessings are wrapped up in computer screens, while others have pretty bows. My company loved me so much that they allowed me to remain part-time working remotely during my time overseas with the option to keep my job upon my return. Spoiler alert: I did not keep my job when I returned.

I remember arriving in the South American country of Belize and seeing the developing infrastructure and homes. It was like the city we had arrived in was in a constant state of construction. More half-built homes than completed ones were everywhere. There were tons of round-a-bouts and two-lane roads, always requiring a U-turn to get anywhere. Since the country was not fully developed, it was like going back in time because of the older, outdated buildings, tangled powerlines, and excessive dirt roads. Nonetheless, I was grateful for the opportunity to be there, and I really could not believe we would get our little taste of somewhat Caribbean life.

When we got into our apartment, it was nice but a little isolating because it was far from the heart of everything. The furniture was quite dated and looked very dingy, but it would have to do. This was my new home, and I knew when I sat on the living room couch with my shoes planted on the cream tile floors, I was not in North Carolina anymore. Soon, Taylor was off to work each morning, and I was stuck in the apartment all day every day, as we only had one car to share. In addition, Belize was not safe enough for internationals, especially women, to travel too much alone. We knew it was not safe when we were awoken the first night to sounds of distant gunshots to later find out there was a hostage takeover that went south. Everything in us wanted to run home, but we stayed.

Alone in my Belize apartment, I was thrust into this space called silence, which was all-engulfing, and it was this place that seemed to get just a bit louder every day.

I would tap ferociously at the keys as I began to plan and develop ideas for my budding company. The days would fly by, as Taylor would return home to me still intently tapping on the keys editing the website I was building for the hundredth time. The quiet of each day from 9:00 a.m. to the cool evenings was one of the greatest experiences I could have ever known. At times, I would miss my family back home, yet I was happy I was blessed to gather ideas from God that I probably would not have heard otherwise had I been busy in the "static" of life. My apartment became a container for ideas, creativity, and dreams. These were things I could never seem to find the time for back at home, even during my times off work. Maybe it was because in Belize, I barely watched television or had stable internet access. I was resolved to focus and chose not to distract myself with retail therapy. Department stores did not need to see me; *I needed to see me* and to hear the voice of God.

At my little, wooden Belize dining room table, I had to deal with myself. I had to face what I did not like about me and my life. I had to face what I really wanted. I had to face who I was and who I wanted to become.

It was painful. It was freeing. It was terrifying. It was exhilarating.

I had never spent so much time listening to my inner thoughts. They had been blocked for so long by television, shopping trips, and other distractions. All this time, I didn't even know my heart's desires in life. I had the chance to begin designing a vision for myself and of what I wanted for now and for the future.

ele

There is a profoundness that comes with owning your silence. I never gave myself permission to question what I wanted out of life and how I wanted to make it happen. It was easy to run to a television binge or to call a friend for a distracting dinner of girl chat. I did not have those choices in Belize, but I had something more. I had time to deal with Sabriya.

We all have brokenness, which forms over time. It is like when a small rock hits your windshield on a car ride and then over time, the windshield begins to crack more and more until one day, you just cannot ignore the crack, and you must get it replaced. Or worse, another rock hits the windshield, and the whole thing shatters. I was the latter. I felt like my perfectionist attitude had run the life out of me—I was in a job I did not want, and I was in a master's degree program that I despised. I never wanted to deal with my junk because I knew then I would have to change, and it was scary. I did not realize the most beautiful part of me was waiting behind the change.

You may be one of those people who feel like you are never good enough. You may feel like you just do not have the smarts or creativity. Maybe you had a rough childhood. You could have been kicked down by life so many times and you are just over it. It is possible that you have been hurt by someone you love and now you are on a downward spiral. Or you could be struggling to get your business off the ground, and it has been too long. While all of those are enough to make you want to sit out on the bench of life, be willing to sit on the bench while listening for the voice of God. He will speak to your heart to help you deal with your circumstances. He will allow you to grieve how you need to grieve. He will allow you to talk it out.

My favorite part is He never judges you but walks you through it. You must spend time with you in order to deal with what happened to you, is happening to you, and will happen for you.

It may feel weird spending time in the silence if you have never done it before, and I want to clarify that this does not mean you never talk. You will talk less and listen more in spaces with no television, no phones, no static, no nothing. You will only take your pen and your journal or scrap paper into your corner of the world. You will write what comes to your heart no matter what you feel in the moment. You will keep doing it over and over, even if you do not hear anything the first few times. You will uncage your thoughts and give them the permission to roam free without limitation or judgement. The silence is freedom from the world's noise to get lost in a place of your own. And most importantly, God dwells in your special space.

Think of your time in the silence as a space to pull you back into your inner self, the higher version of you that knows what you needed all along. Your subconscious was built to house the spirit of your intuition and your truth. There are aspects of religion that may make you feel weak or helpless in the way some people preach it. However, faith is empowering, and God gives you the same power in your spirit that He gave his only son, Jesus Christ. We are made in His image, and we are given the power too.

Just because you are not walking on water or raising others from the dead does not mean you do not have the power to make a major difference in your life and in the lives of others. The silence gives you the ability to pull your spirit from the hectic world who wants to grasp it and never give it back. The silence gives you the power to hear what is unheard and to see the parts of you that you did not have the time to see.

ele

STORYTIME

Looking back on Belize, I pay homage to the woman I used to be— a woman who was afraid to color outside of the lines— a woman who wanted to look the part for everyone else— a woman who wanted to check all the boxes. The woman I used to know, died right there in Belize. The time alone allowed me to reflect on who I was, and it allowed me to spend time figuring out how I could start being in a place of emotional freedom. During the silence, I read books to enhance my faith and my understanding of God and life. I spent time writing and writing away. I spoke to God and asked him all the questions I could ask. I listened closely for answers. A new woman was born.

Slowly but surely, urges and solutions began to come to my heart. I knew they were not of me because they were these grand ideas that came with such powerful vigor. They were bigger than me. They were impossible yet possible all at the very same time. I felt inspired over and over again.

The layers were intoxicating, and I could feel peace and joy spread over my body like waves of fresh air.

I could breathe again. The waves got stronger the more time I spent with God, just us two. I felt safe despite being in one of the more unsafe places to live in the world at the time. Right there in that isolated Belize apartment, I made the decision not to be a victim of my fears and insecurities. I got to be the hero of my own story, and with God, I was going to be the hero of my entire world. Every time my thoughts whispered otherwise, I had the time and peace to consciously move back to the space God wanted me to stay in, confident and empowered.

ele

WHAT DOES THIS MEAN FOR YOU?

Now this is one of the more difficult things for me to explain to you because results will vary. The quality and length of your time in the silence really matters. I understand that you may not be able to access the same type of silence I had for several weeks in Belize, however you can create your own quiet.

Here are a few tips to help you find your own "space of silence:"

- Don't immediately pull into your driveway after work. Park in a local, public area or in a common area of your neighborhood. Spend at least ten minutes with yourself and God. Spend a few minutes saying what you need to say and spend the remaining time listening to your heart and allowing your thoughts to run wild. Keep your thoughts in the present as much as possible.

- Need the quiet in your home? Find a closet or bathroom that people do not use often. Make sure there is enough room for you to sit on the floor. Spend as long as you can with God. Remember, only about 30% talking and 70% listening. Not one speck of silence in your home? Ask a friend if you can use their home. Explain to them you need some time in peace and quiet, and you would like to sit in their bathroom or closet. If it is a good friend, they will understand.

- Late nights and early mornings are some of the quietest times in the world. Try waking up late in the night or early in the morning before the rest of your family is awake. Grab a coffee or your desired pick-me-up and silence away.

- Most important tip: Turn off your phone and all electronic devices, as they can distract you during the silence scenario you choose.

Do not get discouraged if you do not feel different after the first few times in the silence. We will talk more about expectation in faith to help you make your time with God more productive later in this book. You cannot go into the closet with no expectation to find more peace, solutions, and freedom immediately. Your trips into the silence and into your world of hopes and dreams must have intentional meaning. Whether you are going there to seek God and to understand His place in your life more or if you need some answers on a big decision you have to make, go into the silence with a plan in your heart. Give yourself room to receive the answers. They will meet your heart when the time is right, and you must be ready.

When you do finally get to the space you need to be within, you will begin to feel so much peace permeating your day-to-day life. I recommend you try to make time for this space at least once per day. Some of my biggest business decisions come from that silence. As a matter of fact, the silence helped me move my business from below-value pricing to high-end on value pricing because God helped me discover a new tier price structure to implement within my business. *What answers are you seeking right now in business? What has been keeping you up at night? What is keeping you from moving to the next level?*

God + Business Tip #2: One day the words came to my heart: "The more you seek me, the more you will find me." The more you seek God's still voice in the silence, the more you will hear what you need to know. When things happen that shake you up in business, let the silent place become your primary choice. Do not make decisions in fear, stress, or anger. God wants to help you through them if you let Him.

Save this quote to keep you going:

"The silence will be your golden ticket in business. It gives God a direct seat at your table."

CHAPTER 3:
WHO DO YOU THINK YOU ARE ANYWAY?

Here you are trying to put together the pieces of your business, even though you cannot tell what is up from down. You are figuring it out in the best way you can. You know God has touched your heart and you know deep in your bones the work He is calling you to do. Or so you think... you thought you were good until everyone else keeps saying things and asking you questions that remind you just how unqualified you might be.

What did you go to school for? What certifications do you have? How are you an "expert"? Who died and made you the oracle of {insert your product or service here}?

I remember feeling so sick to my stomach every time people would ask me about my experience and how it led me to execute my mental wellness retreat company. I felt automatically like a phony. I felt like I had no business even leading a company. At times, I would talk myself down in conversations saying silly things like: "Yeah, I cannot even believe I am a CEO." You would not believe the babbling and self-deprecation I partook in, desperately trying to stay humble while qualifying myself all in the same sentence. Maybe you are self-taught and do not have an ounce of formal training. Maybe you have formal training in a totally different field, but you transferred the skills. Maybe your life experiences really shaped you and prepared you to lead others. I just listed so many paths, yet every single one of them can leave us thinking that we are completely not prepared to operate a business.

You find yourself scrambling to take every class, every certification, and every program to boost yourself up and to show people that you are in fact qualified. The funny thing is, there is this thing called "imposter syndrome," therefore, no matter what you do to get more qualified, you will never feel qualified enough. It is like chasing your own shadow. No matter how much you run towards it, it will continue to move away from you. There used to be days that I would spend my mornings in the mirror rehearsing my qualifications speech and my "story" to prove to people that I had a right to be there, and I had a right to take up space.

Time to drop a bomb. A BIG one.

Here's the bomb: *No degree, no certification, and no piece of paper can qualify you like God can.* While your credentials are an accomplishment, and they are a great way to expand your skill set, your baseline of qualification lies within you. Everything you need to get started, you already possess. I was not a mental health professional (ironically as I write this book, I am in school for it). I was no health guru. I was definitely not a wellness expert. I was just a woman who had learned some things over the course of her own mental health battles and believed there was a creative way to bring wellness solutions into someone else's life outside of standard treatments. I started with what I knew and worked on growing and expanding from there. God qualified me from the start, therefore, people started listening to me. That is how I got amazing organizations, individuals, and companies to trust Project Passport with their time and money, even though I was an unknown brand.

I am in no way telling you to pretend or to act like you are qualified for things that you are not. You cannot pose as a mental health professional or a medical doctor. You cannot pose as a lawyer or any professional in a certified field unless you hold those credentials. You find out where you can start with what you do have, and if you want to expand your legal reach and abilities, then you can consider getting the certifications or degrees you desire. For example, I chose a life coaching and personal development focus because the field is flexible and does not require set credentials for you to practice. My educational background, creativity, unique skill set, and personal experiences was enough to get me started.

God provides you with the raw resources to chisel out your start, and when God has His hand on it, the pathway is atypical of this world. With Him, you create a lane that does not exist for anyone but you. I am sure people in the Bible believed Noah, Mary, and David were all crazy because they did things and experienced things outside of this world.

For instance, Noah created something that did not exist—a boat to house every animal pair in the world to be exact. David did something that had never been done before. He defeated a giant with a simple stone. Mary had a baby, even though she was a virgin (turned out He was the one and only Jesus Christ). God does not ask you to do things people would expect. This is going to be the hardest part of your journey as you fight what the world expects from you versus what God has called you to do. Are you listening to Him or making up excuses based on the credentials you don't have?

STORYTIME

This idea was bursting through my head and heart, and though I knew it was completely insane, I just had to do it. I had just launched Project Passport, my mental wellness retreat and event company in early 2019, and here I was trying to piece together my own women's conference event. I had barely attended any women's conferences myself, nor had I ever planned one, but I was going to plan my own conference event anyway. I had no venue, no audience, no speakers, no theme, and I had no idea where to start. I was nervous, yet I was more excited than I had been in a very long time. I decided to consult a mentor for help before I got started.

To my surprise, some of the first words out of my mentor's mouth were somewhere along the lines of: *"A conference event? Who is going to be your keynote speaker? No one will come if you do not invest in a well-known speaker."* My heart fluttered in shock. I had not expected that response, as I thought she would be happy and supportive of my idea. Immediately, I began to almost regret the whole thing. I quickly explained how I planned to keynote the event myself and to bring in someone else to speak, maybe a panel of everyday women of some sort. I wanted the event to be about real women of the community and not some fancy, big names. I wanted it to be down-to-earth and genuine, like my business model. She insisted that if I did not have a well-known speaker, it probably would not be worth my time. She remarked, *"Conferences do not make much money anyways."* My spirit dropped. *"But* it is not about the money," I insisted. "It is about the impact and showing people what my new company is all about." Nothing I said mattered, as her lack of faith in me was all over her face, and I was mortified. Our relationship was never the same after that, and it is practically non-existent to this day.

Who do you think you are, Sabriya? Trying to put together a conference event and no one knows or even cares about you. Those words kept whirling through my head. These were new negative thoughts I had not known before the conversation with my ex-mentor. I knew my family and friends would show up, but outside of that, it would be an empty room. Maybe she's right, I thought, who do I think I am? Something in me overpowered that voice like a fire out of the pit of my soul. It told me to do it anyway. So, I did.

In August 2019, after months of preparing, designing my own decorations and centerpieces by hand, picking the right venue (fortunately, I used my fiancé's mom's church at no cost), decorating the space with my dad for two days straight, working tirelessly to attract speakers and panelists, organizing catering (which flopped!), and organizing a dessert and drink bar, a conference was happening. I barely had the budget to make it happen, yet I made this event look as if it was a featured page on the front of the most amazing Pinterest account. Oh, I was so proud! We sold out every single one of our event tickets (40+ tickets) to people who were not just friends and family. Throughout, I prayed to God for the right words and for people to show up, and it was a dream come true.

I did it. With the help of loved ones, I hosted and keynoted my first-ever conference event called, TransformHER. You can look it up and find it on my company website if you want to see how it went with your own eyes. My first-ever team member, Hannah, was right beside me in making this event a success. Who did I think I was? I was SABRIYA AHNISHKA DOBBINS baby, period! I was someone who told my story on that stage, and I was someone who had something to say to help these women live better and to help them thrive. Thinking about this moment has me overjoyed because that day changed my life forever. I had actually forgotten my notes for my keynote in the car on the day of the event.

At first, I was freaking out, however it did not matter because the words poured out as I spoke with confidence and power. After my keynote address, I remember looking over at my aunt, who provided free photography for me during the event, saying, *"I need to feel this forever. This is where I am supposed to be in life. This is what I have been waiting for all along."* She smiled at me and nodded and said, *"You can make it happen."*

This experience taught me that if I decided to let someone else decide who I was, then I would have never been afforded my life-changing moment. I would have never been able to create something so beautiful for the women of TransformHER. I would have allowed someone else to qualify who I was meant to be in my craft.

The moment I decided to say "yes" to what I knew I was in my heart was the moment I started living in my purpose.

~ell~

I wish I could tell you this was a one-time incident, and everything went happily ever after. There have been so many more times where I have been challenged in who I am and what I can bring to the table. People have pushed me to move my company style and brand into a direction they believed was best for me. People have suggested I stop or start things that I don't believe in doing. People have even asked me to call myself titles, which do not define me. I am a Head Retreat Leader and Life Discovery Expert because God told me so, and I am proud to be it. You are a {insert the titles true to your heart here} because God said so!

I even got to a point where I thought my story was not as dramatic as all of the other life coaches out there. They had some rags to riches experience, and this just did not define me. Many of them had highly traumatic stories, and those did not fit me either. God reminded me it did not matter. My story and my experiences of perfectionism, depression, anxiety, and imposter syndrome (feeling like you are not good enough) were just what the right people needed to hear to thrive on their own journeys. They needed my story to help them rediscover their own hope. God showed me time and time again that a "dramatic story" was not what made me. It was being the authentic me in the sea of "perfect people," and this made people want to know what I could do to help them.

I continue to grow my knowledge base, and this may result in more degrees or certifications. However, the difference is that these are things I am pursuing for *me*. I am growing more out of my passion and desire to learn. These credentials happen to support the optics of the world standards of "qualified," yet I do not put my faith in them. I know God will touch the heart of the clients who need to hear from me most, and no degree or certificate will keep them from working with me, ever.

At the end of the day, you are exactly who you believe you are. People will challenge you. They will want you to follow a lane that is not your own. They will make you feel inadequate according to their standards. Read that again: *according to their standards*. That does not mean you have to allow yourself to crumble. There are so many game changers and leaders in this world who do not have a degree or certification to do what they do. There is no need for me to run down the laundry list of people without degrees who have experienced great success to get my point across. Besides, you do not need the list to qualify yourself wherever you are. You need to be willing to trust that God will place you in the right situation for the right people. I once heard Lisa Nichols, a famous speaker say, *"Your 70% may be someone's 100%."* You may think what you know is not much, but your level of knowledge may be their fresh start.

As you level up and choose to obtain the credentials to expand your own knowledge, you will naturally gain more rapport and credibility, and this is a byproduct of your effort in the world. Remember however, one credential does not define you. Even before the credential, you still mattered, and you still had something to say. God said you were set to do this before the greater world said it. Give yourself the credit you deserve.

~~ele~~

WHAT DOES THIS MEAN FOR YOU?

I once wrote a blog called *"Death to Checkboxes"* for the Project Passport *Living Life Full Force* blog, and it explained how I was a slave to checkboxes my whole life and how it was time to stop. I had recently dropped out of a Master's of Business Administration (MBA) program, which was a waste of my time and money because I hated the focus, and I knew I was getting the degree because it "looked good." I want you to ask yourself a few questions:

- Is your career and life truly a journey or is it just a slew of checkboxes that look good to have?

- When you make major business or career decisions, are they based on your genuine interest or because they seem to make sense with what society says?

- Is the glory of what people will say about your accomplishment more exciting than your own joy? Think really hard about this one because we often lie to ourselves here.

- How far are you willing to go to fulfill your {insert your treasured loved ones}'s dreams for you over your own? Have you morphed their dreams into your own?

I suggest you start separating the parts of you from the parts that others have put on you. You will never be everything for everyone no matter how hard you try. If you cannot make choices based on your own personal journey, then God cannot show you His immense plan for you. It is like accepting a mini cupcake upfront when if you just waited a little while longer, you would have received a lifetime subscription to a gourmet bakery.

You may feel frustrated because you are taking your time in pursuing further credentials and titles, but you will be proud of yourself when you slow down and choose things that are just right for your growth.

God wants you to succeed beyond your wildest dreams in this life and in the next with Him. If He has something for you, it is going to be for you and the world does not get to decide if you are good enough. He has already promised this so many times in the Bible with my favorite verse being: *"For I know the plans I have for you,"* declares the LORD, *"plans to prosper you and not to harm you, plans to give you hope and a future"* (Jeremiah 29:11). That verse alone should get you through the day-to-day because if you truly contemplate it, and if you truly believe it, God will show up and show out in your life. I know it because I am living it daily.

God + Business Tip #3: No one gets to qualify you in this life like God does. Even if you are not sure where to start, put together a prototype of your product/service based on what you know. You would be surprised by what you can pre-sell based on what you do know and how quickly you will determine how to fill in the gaps with research and prayer.

Save this quote to keep you going:

"Unlike the world, God knows exactly who you are supposed to be. It's faith over face-value for the win."

CHAPTER 4:
IT IS NOT A MATTER OF IF...

Whether you are in the early stages of your business or if you have been in it for a while, doubts will always appear as you wonder if your product or service will do well in your respective market. You are constantly facing unknowns with clients, vendors, and you are in moments where you have no control on whether things will work out or not. Sometimes you wait months for outcomes, good or bad, and sometimes you wait years. With a bit of tweaking and editing, you could shorten the wait from years to months to days, but you must be willing to put the product out there first.

I spent a lot of the early days in my business waiting, waiting for clients to buy, waiting for a "yes," waiting for the phone to ring. There were many days it did not ring. In fact, those first months of retreat sales were brutal because I did not get a single call or email for weeks. When I would get a phone call, my whole heart would jump as I babbled away to clients with nervous energy clouding my voice. I sometimes forgot important facts about the retreats because I was so excited just to have anyone who cared!

After not receiving an inkling of success, I started to flounder. Then, I remember something I had learned in church over the years. God already had a powerful and positive outcome laid out for me. I just had to live as someone who was planning on these outcomes materializing. I could not function from a place of hope but a place of expectation. Just as much as I could expect something bad to happen, I had to prepare for something good to happen. I had to move from a place of IF someone calls to WHEN someone calls. This meant taking two breaths before I answered the phone and having my notes ready. I had to make plans for WHEN someone booked rather than IF someone booked. I began drafting follow-up emails to send clients after they booked the retreat. Sure enough, within a few weeks of changing my mindset from IF to WHEN, I received my first client booking. I was ecstatic. I remember exactly where I was, and the moment I checked my email. At first, I thought my dad had bought a shirt since he was one of my only clients, but no, someone else had actually booked a spot on the Kenya travel retreat! And it was not a person I knew! While we love it when friends and family support us, it hits different when someone you don't know believes in your business.

Preparing for the WHEN in your business is powerful because it allows you to create a prosperity magnet. God knows you believe He is going to help you; therefore, He places a spirit of belief in your clients to choose you. If you have not fully prepared materials for your clients and you are hoping someone will book your services, while deep down you do not have faith, then you are stabbing yourself in the foot as you walk. You are your own cinder block shoes. You must ask yourself the questions: *What happens when someone buys my product? Will I be prepared to give them a good customer service experience?* If you do not have a basket to catch your clients successfully, then why would anything fly your way?

ele

STORYTIME

The pandemic had not hit yet, and I was in the early part of 2020 meeting with a representative from the Durham National Alliance of Mental Illness (NAMI). I was so nervous because after attending networking event after event, I did not appear to make any real impactful connections. My company was not getting much traction, and I began to question if I had made the right choice and if I was really cut out for this. What if people saw through me and believed I had no idea what I was talking about? Perhaps, I actually did not have any idea what I was talking about. The doubts were coming from the left and right. Fortunately, the last event I attended allowed me to connect with the NAMI board member, and she seemed really interested in what I was doing with my budding company. I was scheduled to meet her at a Starbucks coffee shop about forty-five minutes from my home at the time, and I was praying the meeting would be worth the drive.

My hands clenched the steering wheel, as I navigated a new area of town. I whispered a small prayer asking God if this was my chance, an opportunity to manifest my destiny. I nervously walked in anticipating her arrival at the crowded coffee shop. It was even more nerve-wracking because I felt like everyone was staring at me as I sat at the table alone. After a few minutes, she walked in with her sweet son, whom she had revealed prior to our meeting, had autism. She sat down and got her son settled in with his snacks and began to share a bit about herself.

I smiled eagerly with a goofy grin and my Project Passport folder of materials in hand. We began communicating about the importance of mental health and wellbeing. We agreed on our frustration with the current systems in place and how we knew there was so much to be done. My nerves began to fade as I found my flow in our passionate conversation. As we talked, out of nowhere, she stopped mid-speech and looked at me in a peculiar way. I was startled, as I was not sure what was happening. She cocked her head to the side ever so slightly, looked at me directly in the eyes and she said:

"God has something really amazing for you. You are going to change the mental health space and make a greater impact than you know. Yes, I feel it on my heart. He is showing me. You are exactly what the world is needing."

She nodded her head vigorously and looked at me with pure conviction. My eyes were so wide with surprise, terror, and gratitude, all wrapped in one. All I could do was break into a shy smile and respond with sheer appreciation. It was what I needed to hear to know that I was on the right track. She had changed my world just right there in that busy Starbucks coffee shop.

She had no idea what I had been going through when it came to my doubts, lack of progress, and fears, yet she was telling me the outcome I desired. How was it possible that a woman I barely knew could tell me I was going to make it? The only explanation was God. I knew it from the bottom of my heart. God will speak through situations, people, and in ways you would not expect to let you know He is rooting for you. I know it was God who spoke through this beautiful woman because He continues to do this to me every time I experience doubt in my business.

One day I would panic about how things might not work, and the next day I would be chosen for a blog or article feature. Another day I would start second guessing my abilities, and the next day, a random client would email me saying how much they just appreciated the experience they had with my team and how it changed their life. It is like God tells you to stop in your tracks when you get on that "IF-train." He reminds you that you need to live in the "when" daily. In the meantime, little victories happen along the way to WHEN-ville.

Later, the same lady from the coffee shop would be an integral part of the turning point of Project Passport from just trying to make it, to a true success. She elevated me in her community as much as possible. She referred business my way anytime she could. She got grants for me to really make my work happen on a larger scale. She listened to me on those days I felt doubt and encouraged me. She had and continues to have total faith in me, and she helps me believe I will change the world. I am doing just that, and she is still cheering me on. I love you Jackie! Get you a Jackie too. We all need at least one!

ele

Expectation is a powerful aspect of your entrepreneurship journey and you must take it seriously. You must plan for things to work in your favor. We will get more into how to pray with expectation in the next chapter. However, I want to make something clear. You must know when to stop and re-route while still using the spirit of expectation. If aspects of your product or services are not doing well and you do not make the proper changes, you will not get the results you want. While you are planning for blessings to happen, you have to give your best work in the process.

God rewards those who work diligently for Him, and He will not reward an aimless project, one where you have not put the work into it. One thing that frustrates me is when people preach that God will give them everything they need if they just wait. This only considers one aspect of the instructions. The Bible clearly states: *"For as the body without the spirit is dead, so faith without works is dead also,"* James 2:26. Your WHEN will never come IF you do not do the work required of you. You must do both.

One thing I want to address is the thought that success in finances is a bad gift from Satan and not God. Some people have been preaching the message of "starving in the name of God" for way too long. This has caused people to freeze in fear of success and wealth. I know I have. Isn't that something? Being afraid of actually succeeding! There are verses throughout the Bible where God rewarded those who worked hard and followed His will financially and in resources. He is excited to reward you in this life. He simply asks us not to worship or tie ourselves into the material things and to honor Him in the process. I used to be terrified of success because I thought it would make me a bad person. Now I realize, it is a byproduct of following God's will for my life.

Do not sit back and hope things will fall onto your plate. Use the creativity and resources God has given you to be a part of the outcome. Invest in ads that are good and relevant to your business needs. Continue networking with new and potential partners. Ensure your accounting is done by the right person. Consider updating your website. Do the work it takes and expect it to work out at the same time. God will reward your efforts if you keep your eyes on Him. Do not focus on the "if;" focus on the "when."

~ele~

WHAT DOES THIS MEAN FOR YOU?

This is an opportunity for you to do a mental audit on your business. You should test yourself to determine if you really believe {insert your business name here} is going to make it. Take some time to complete the tasks below:

1. Test your systems. Take yourself through the entire client process from initial interest to checkout to post-purchase. What does it look like? Is it choppy on the back end? Will you be able to deliver the service or product in sufficient time and with quality? This will help you decide whether you live in IF-ville or WHEN-ville. Make sure you are preparing to receive clients.

2. Watch your words. Check to see if you keep using a contingency in everything you say about the outcomes of your business. The words "If, maybe, perhaps," are great examples. Consider what things would look like should you say the word "when" in place of "if." How are you describing your future business success to your team, to others, and to yourself?

3. Write your vision. You may have already written it, but I want you to write it again. Think about the overall goals and outcomes that you want to occur through your company's mission. What emotions do you feel when you write it? Do you even believe it? Ask yourself if you feel doubt just writing those words. Ask yourself why you feel those doubts. Determine how you can replace those doubts with expectations for positive outcomes even in the face of the "unknown."

4. Believe in your outcome. Understand that even with the WHEN mindset, you may not get the outcome you expected. The best part is that the new outcome is usually going to be better when you know God is in on it. Believe in a good or massively better outcome no matter what it looks like. Even if the initial outcome feels a bit iffy, it may be an opportunity for you to innovate to create a more dynamic result. Or the outcome can take you in a whole new direction like I experienced with my company and when I launched a successful virtual division that was never in my plans to begin with. While I was afraid when the pandemic occurred and had no idea what things would look like, I knew the outcome was going to work exactly how it needed to (after I got out of my emotional rut, of course!) It was just a matter of time, and it worked according to God's plan.

When you change your mindset, your business will begin to flow differently. Time is your best friend in this process because as long as you are alive and well, you still get to see the beautiful outcomes. God may not work at the speed you want, however you will appreciate the perfect speed He has for you. For example, prior to the pandemic, had my company pre-booked a ton of in-person retreats as quickly as I'd wanted, I would have been bankrupt. It was already difficult to provide the pandemic refunds for my retreat to Kenya. I would have had to refund more money while trying to get refunds from vendors. God's perfect timing for bookings saved me from a world of hurt in the long run. The fact that I had obtained retreat bookings at all gave me the hope I needed to create a new virtual product with my team.

Things may not play out in the exact process you expect, but each aspect has a lesson or new direction that you need to pursue to narrow down into the place God has created for you. And believe me, this place is often where everyone else is not and is exactly where you need to be. God reveals divine spaces and gaps in the world that only your business can fill. I can promise you this to be true because He did it for me. God wants you to believe through Him, you WILL fill your divine spaces when the timing is right.

God + Business Tip #4: When you are organizing and planning in business, you need to establish a game plan for *when* your projects are a success. If you try to sell something with your hands and teeth clenched, you will get exactly what you expect deep down– nothing. Expect a long-haul experience but know the outcome is guaranteed because God has already approved it.

Save this quote to get you through:

"It is not a matter of if, it is a matter of when."
-Unknown

ele

WHAT'S NEXT?

You are now about to enter Part II of this book. Part I was the critical foundation to your business. Each chapter shared a special component that should now become the proverbial base to your business: Faith as Fuel, The Silence, Who You Are, and Living in the When. These components will serve as a key combination for your new or renewed business. The first few chapters should have helped you develop foundational markers on what makes your business powerful with a tool greater than any human on this earth—the greatness of God.

Part II will focus on the concept of faith and how to incorporate it into the art of running your business. As you know, faith is the most impressive weapon in your entrepreneurial tool kit, yet it takes time to work that muscle. It takes intention and commitment even when you are tired. Faith is more than just believing in yourself; it is knowing that you have the number one team player in your company– God. He is the most dedicated, supportive, loyal, and innovative team player you will ever know. And to your relief, he never quits, ever.

PART II: THE PURSUIT OF FAITH

In faith, everything and anything is possible.

CHAPTER 5:
PRAYERS FROM THE LAND OF EXPECTATION

Quick question: Do you pray? It is possible that you pray all the time, or you only pray right before bed. You may never have prayed a day in your life. I am not here to judge you. Believe it or not, many people are praying but they are not *really* praying. You might be one of them. I was one of them. Most of my prayers were about as authentic as those fake nails I sometimes wear. I look back at those half-hearted prayers I made, and I completely understand why some of them did not pan out how I wanted. I was never really praying with an ounce of *expectation*. In other words, I prayed for things that I did not expect to happen for me. We talked about IF and WHEN in the last chapter, but this chapter will discuss how to put expectation into action.

Imagine this prayer by your bedside: *"Dear God, I really want to find success in my business. I hope I can make $100,000 in sales next year (*says "yeah right" in my head*). God, please let these clients trust me. (*says "haha real funny... why would they" in my head*) And God, I just want to change the world, so please use me. (*says "who do I think I am, Martin Luther King, or what" in my head*) Amen."*

If you read this paragraph and it sounded just like your internal dialogue and prayers, you are not alone. Many of us pray with this whole "reality check" driving our entire process, causing us to lose faith in ourselves and what God can do for us. While we may live in the physical world, we are of God, therefore, we are not of this world.

There is a greatness, which has been encoded in your DNA long before you were even born, carved by God just for you. However, many of us completely forget and allow the physical world to paint our lens of reality.

In God's spiritual world, anything is possible. God's world is here, there, and everywhere. There is this Bible verse I am obsessed with because not only does it apply to Heaven, but I believe it applies to the works that are yet to come from those who love Him on earth. Here's how it goes: *"Eye hath not seen, nor ear heard, nor have entered into the heart of man the things which God has prepared for those who love Him* (1 Corinthians 2:9)."

The verse explains those who love God are going to be able to experience fruits and create ideas that are unseen and unheard to this world. Therefore, if you are making your decisions solely on what you see and hear from others on this earth, you are severely withholding your opportunities to receive greatness beyond what the hearts of man can imagine. You must expect divine opportunities and miracles to take place in your business. You cannot let what is in front of you always define what you think your outcome will be.

When you get on an airplane, do you get on it expecting it not to make it to the next destination? Do you assume that your plane is going to go down? You must have at a minimum, some level of confidence that the plane is going to make it because you would not get on it in the first place if you didn't. Who really says it will though? Did the pilot personally come and tell you they are fully experienced, ready to fly, and feeling mentally well to get you where you need to be? No. You simply have faith that the pilot is mentally well, and they are going to get you there safely to the best of their ability.

The same faith you place in the pilot as you sit on the plane preparing for what is going to happen in order to reach your destination, should be the same faith (and then some) that you apply when you pray to God seeking your next steps. You are expecting Him to answer. You are going to start preparing that website for the new product ideas. You are going to set your prices for those sponsors who will come. You are preparing to disembark your business decision plane at the perfect destination hand-designed by God. You must expect that the answers you seek, will be found and the clarity you need is about to appear.

God knows when you are stalling. He can tell when you are trying to tiptoe around your prayers because you are not really saying them with conviction, and you do not plan for Him to answer. Then you wake up day after day flabbergasted that your situation has not yet changed. Truthfully speaking, by default you have allowed yourself to join Satan's team of doubt and despair. Satan loves it when you doubt God. He loves that you do not think God will answer your prayers. He takes those actions as concurrence with him and because you gave him the door, sometimes Satan can be the one who answers your prayers. Initially, everything appears to be alright, and you think you are getting what you want. In the next moment, your life is a rollercoaster of Hell on earth. When you are in the space of doubt, you start hijacking decisions that God, the better team player, can help you make in business, and you hurt your outcomes.

STORYTIME

It is late 2020 and I am navigating this new virtual retreat space. I sat on the floor praying to God that I will be able to get a client to buy a company retreat. Deep down, I felt like a total phony. I was just some bachelor's degree girl, and I barely spent more than a few years in the corporate world. I honestly felt like I was asking for a longshot with God. Part of me knew that I did not even believe my own prayer. Why would another client trust me? Even the clients who did choose to work with me I made excuses for. I could not accept that I was qualified and cut out for this. I kept believing they did not have better options, so they settled with me each and every time. All these negative beliefs interrupted my prayers viciously, and sure enough, I was confronted with weeks of empty telephone and email inboxes.

Then, I had a thought. What if I expected something good to happen in life with the same energy that I used being afraid of a bad outcome. As much as I was expecting clients not to book with me, why couldn't I pray with an expectation that through God, it was going to happen one way or the other? What if I just stopped making this about me and what I did not have, and I made it more about God and what I know He could do through me? I began praying a new prayer with a new tune.

I explained to God how I knew He worked miracles in the Bible through Jesus. I know He has done so many amazing things through the lives of others, even when they were not ready or did not possess the skills. I told Him I expected Him to do it for me because I have His will to live out. I purposely blocked the doubts trying to creep into my head. Every time doubt surfaced, I crushed it with a quick diversion back to prayer.

I spent time visualizing with God what things would look like when I reached my goals and expectations. I could feel the breeze of the beautiful beach home. I could see the smiles on the clients' faces. I could see the emails of gratitude for what our team has done for another company's team. I began to spend half of my prayer time praying and the other half, exploring my world of expectation. I began to experience a world of WHEN things happened for me, rather than IF they would. Refer back to Chapter 4 if you need a refresher on IF and WHEN.

The beauty of my life changing felt almost instantaneous. Bookings started to come, and they began to come fast. Before I knew it, just as the holidays approached, more clients booked my services in a month's time than we had received since we began company retreats just a few months earlier. I knew the bookings were coming even before they came. My confidence had become so deeply nestled with God to the point that He began to show me transactions in my dreams before they had even occurred! In one instance, I distinctly remember seeing the letters of a client's name in my dream. While I could not remember the dream fully the next morning, a client called me by that exact name ready to book a package. It was the largest company retreat package I had ever booked at the time. Those dreams do not always come but when they do, I am forever grateful God gave me that little bit of insight to remind me that I am going the right way.

ele

I wish I could give you a magic formula on how to expect God to do things for you, but it is a choice. Just as you choose to believe in Jesus Christ as your Savior, as I hope you do (the most rewarding thing EVER), you must choose to believe He will be there for you. How are you going to accept Him in your heart and not think He is going to want to change your life for the better? God is ready and willing to bring you joy. He loves us just that much. We cannot expect Him to leave us in the dirt.

Do you expect your feet to stay on the ground and believe gravity will not take you away from Earth? Do you expect the moon will not touch the ground? Do you expect that if you jump into water, you will become wet? The same conviction you have for those questions must be the same conviction you use when you pray.

Okay, you may be reading this and thinking, *I have no idea how to pray or if I am praying right.* There is no right way to pray. You can pray while driving. You can pray while on your knees by the bed. You can pray as you sit at your office desk. You can pray in the middle of a large soccer game with your eyes open. You have a direct line from your heart to God and He hears through all the noise. It is simply a conversation you would have with a trusted friend. You want to give praise about the great things you appreciate from the friend, and you want to let them know what you need or where you are struggling. That is it.

If you are still a bit unsure where to start, I recommend you write a letter to God and read it aloud. There is something about praying out loud that feels powerful to me. I think when I say the words aloud, I am putting them out there with full confidence God is hearing them. When I say them aloud, instead of under my breath, they feel more real, and I feel like God can scoop them up in happiness, as He knows I am leaning on His wisdom. I am willing to look like a crazy person and talk aloud to God anywhere and anytime. I expect that my words are being heard, and before my very own eyes, I have seen the outcomes from those prayers.

"But my prayers did not get answered! I expected God to do "X" for my business, but it did not happen!" These words are bound to come from your mouth from time to time. Yes, some of the prayers you ask for will not get answered in the way you want. However, understand this. Every prayer is answered. Either it is going to happen the way you want, it will not happen at all, or it may happen in a way you did not expect. An outcome still counts as an answer. Just because it is not the one you prayed and planned for does not mean God does not love you any less or does not hear you. Sometimes, an alternative answer or a "no" is what you need before you know you need it. That "no" could have been the one thing you needed to evolve your vision to the greater one God called it to be. That alternative outcome could have ended up being the best thing for you and your business. Remember my story about the pandemic turning my business inside out? While travel retreats were a "no," we blossomed in the virtual space creating financial stability that we needed more than anything.

No matter what happens, God has your best interest at heart. He says it over and over in the Bible. He treats us like princes and princesses on this earth if you just let Him. One of my favorite verses that reminds me just how much he treats us like royalty:

"You are with me; Your rod and Your staff, they comfort me. You prepare a table before me in the presence of my enemies. You anoint my head with oil; my cup overflows. Surely goodness and mercy will follow me all the days of my life, and I will dwell in the house of the LORD forever (Psalm 23:4-6)."

He has got me covered through thick and thin, so when I do not get the immediate outcomes I want, I know they will make sense in time.

⁓ele⁓

WHAT DOES THIS MEAN FOR YOU?

So now you are praying away on all those dreams and goals that you have set for your business? Wonderful! But you need to check yourself. You need to make sure you are praying with two things in mind:

1. Is what you are asking for going to give glory to God?

While there is no wrong way to pray, you can pray for the wrong things. Prayers to hurt, cheat, or do wrong by others are not healthy prayers. They are not prayers that capture the essence of what God wants for you. Conniving Satan can sneak in on those unhealthy prayers and like a genie say, "Your wish is my command." You and I both know how many of those genie stories end up– worse off than you were before, and then you realize you did not need the genie at all. Ensure you are praying with positive intent around what you are asking for. If you must take from others in a negative way to get what you want, it is probably not the right prayer. God already said he was preparing a seat for you. There is a spot with your nametag at the table. You do not have to take the seat of others to get yours. This is not musical chairs, while I do love that game.

2. Do you really believe He can help you achieve the prayer?

You must really work your faith muscle with this expectation of prayers. The best way to help in building this expectation meter is to get specific with your prayers. Detail every aspect you are asking for in your life from how you want to feel, what you want to see, hear, smell, etc. The more detailed you make it, the more committed you are to it, and the more you can help create expectation with God. If you are taking the time to explain all these details to Him, then you have greater belief in the fact that these things can happen for you.

If you can answer those two questions comfortably, then you are well on your way to watching your business and life transform before your very eyes. God will start putting ideas, solutions, and creations in your head that you could have never imagined. One day, you will look back in sheer joy and shock saying, "Wow, I really am here!" You will know deep down what it took to get there.

God + Business Tip #5: When you pray with clarity, expecting God's glory to reign over your business, do not be surprised when your baskets start to overflow. Make sure you are set up to receive the rain of

blessings on your business because the showers are coming. In addition to prayer, being prepared shows God that you really do believe He has got you covered. Do you have your blessings catcher ready?
Save this quote to get you through:

"You must pray for your dreams with the same confidence you have that the sun will rise another day."

CHAPTER 6:
THE BETTER HALF OF YOUR BUSINESS

Operating a business can be lonely. Nothing can truly ever prepare you for the weight entrepreneurship bears. As I said before, I read all of the books, listened to many of the podcasts, and answered all those pre-business questions, but it is nothing like you would ever expect. Things happen, you are thrown left and right into so many situations, and sometimes you stare at the crossroads before you in total fear. There are moments you are desperate to turn to anyone to help you figure out these tough situations. I am here to tell you that they are not for you to figure out alone. God raised His hand to become your business partner the moment you decided to start your business.

You may have other partners in your business or maybe you are a solopreneur. It does not matter which one applies to you, as the most knowledgeable and dedicated partner is God. He works for your business even when you are off, taking breaks, asleep, or just downright aloof. Isn't it a relief to know your operations are still going on even when you are not in the midst of running them? Maybe it does not feel that way because you are not getting many phone calls or work is slow. Do not be fooled by those things. God is, in fact, working.

He is busy planting seeds into the right hearts of the right clients. He is helping create new ideas in your head to make business run more smoothly. He is busy inspiring future employees who will believe in your vision with their whole hearts. He is helping speed up your work by putting your mind into "flow," setting the energy just right. He is making the right connections, so the perfect person pops up in your social media feed or shows up at the networking event you are planning to attend. He is orchestrating a symphony for your business, which may look invisible to the naked eye, yet, if you tap into your spirit, the music will blow your mind. It will be the most beautiful sound you will ever hear.

I have read many books and articles about this wonderful concept I carry in my heart daily: "Co-creating with God." Whenever I must make big decisions in business, I turn inward to the spirit of Him, which lives within me to ask for clarity. And sure enough, if I am patient enough, the answer comes to my heart one way or the other.

Remember when you were a kid in school and you had to do group projects? The teacher would call the names of who is in whose group, and people would either cheer or groan at the thought of working with their new teammates. Sometimes you had relief because you were being paired with the "smart" kids in your class. Sometimes you cringed in fear because you knew you were stuck with the class "slackers." I loved group projects because I was usually the one who took the lead, and it was a creative opportunity for me. Okay and I also admit because I was a bit bossy. Okay, really bossy. Nonetheless, there were the team members who were lazy and never did their part, leaving me with late nights I would dread. This was my life in college, too, but worse. I had such a leading spirit, yet it was always accompanied by a price. We were going to do good on this project or I was going to die trying for us all! I was ready to ride – dawn, noon, or midnight!

Imagine this new narrative. Your business is a gigantic group project; however this project's team composition is different. It is the dream team; the best team you have ever been on. It is composed of you, perhaps some business partners, your mentors, anyone else who you trust to support you and oh, the most important day one team member there is... God. There is something interesting about this {new} team member because He seems to have all the best ideas. In fact, the ideas are sheer perfection, and they are exactly what you need when you need them. He shows up on time every day to work with you. He works overtime. He picks up your slack. Bottom line, He just seems to constantly push out the perfect information when you are in a bind. God is like the "smart" kid of your group project times one million.

When I recruited God to join Project Passport as a VIP, C-Suite member, my business ran differently. While I know He placed the idea on my heart, I had to allow Him to be in on it to make it happen. My business did not feel of this world because it simply was not. It was an enlightened business that lived on its own plane of the world. This did not mean I did not face obstacles, but I felt more equipped when I faced them with God on my side as my new co-founder.

ele

STORYTIME

Remember the lady from NAMI whom I met at Starbucks (I mentioned her in the last chapter)? As I shared, she continued to be a huge part of my journey to success. She was constantly encouraging me to trust myself and God in the process, especially when my faith began to waiver when the pandemic hit. I had lost so much, as all my clients had to be refunded for the travel retreat I had booked for them. Now you know I was able to turn this around and build a virtual business, but what you do not know is that it did not happen because I got over myself and pulled up my bootstraps. In fact, I wallowed for weeks and cried like a baby constantly. I slept my days away, and I tried to distract myself with silly television shows to block the pain. Whether I was watching families clash on 90 Day Fiance' or fighting monsters on Legacies, I wanted to deal with any reality but my own. I prayed but they were shaky prayers in which I often ended abruptly. I was not sure how God aka: my business-partner-assuming-the-world-was-not-in-a-pandemic was going to assist me through this one.

Oh Jackie. The lady who changed my world in a coffee shop that day. After a few months into pandemic mode, I called her on the telephone explaining just how defeated I felt. I was embarrassed to admit to anyone outside of my family that my company was crumbling. Multiple times, I considered just shutting down so I would not hemorrhage any more money on a travel company like mine, one that was no longer relevant. I could barely tell my team the truth because I knew how disappointed they would be. She calmly said something to me over the phone along the lines of: *"Do this virtual thing. You can do it. God is going to help you figure out how to make it happen. You are going to break barriers and create something amazing if you do it. You have the talent and the ability."* Immediately I thought:

"*Okay, Jackie, easier said than done.*" She was so positive about it all, and to be honest, the feeling was not mutual. I almost wanted to be angry at her for even thinking I could survive this. My eyes brimmed with hot tears and my cheeks burned in distress.

I was so adamant that virtual just would not work for the highly interactive retreat experience my business would bring to the table. Yet, this woman had once again planted a seed in my last waking hour. Once again, somehow, she was pulling me off the ledge. What kind of magic was this woman on? God's, of course! It did not stop with her.

One of my dear mentors told me, "*Sabriya, your company is so young, which makes you agile. That is your strength.*" All I could think was, "*Agile? How in the world was I going to be agile with nothing? Big, rich companies who have their stuff together are agile! Me? I am dead in the water.*" Lore, my mentor, did not mince words and she said what she said. She insisted I would figure this out. I wanted to scream. Why was she so sure? Who did she think she was? Looking back, I had such a bratty mind. I was in my wallowing and these amazing, warrior women knew better than me. Overcoming so much in their own lives, they did not see it any different for me.

How was everyone else I trusted so confident I was going to figure this mess out but me? What did they know? They were not in my shoes. God knew that speaking to me through my own head and heart was not going to cut it. As my life business partner, He took matters into His own hands to instill confidence in me through two women I trusted immensely in my business decisions. Despite a pandemic, these ladies believed without a waiver or doubt that my company was going to thrive, even though I had lost everything. Surely, this was divine intervention. At that point, I knew if these two unrelated women saw something in me and my business, clearly it was there. Clearly, it was something I could not see. God knew they were the push I needed to just jump. I jumped and I did not look back because the only way I could go was forward. I am forever grateful for those women in my life because they allowed themselves to speak the messages into me that God wanted me to hear, yet my mind had refused to listen. He works overtime behind the scenes.

ele

ANOTHER STORYTIME

I had just finished an appointment with a nice lady in a shop all the way across town. She ran retreats herself and wanted to meet me to see if there was any room for collaboration. I was always eager to network. Even though it had been a far drive, I was glad I went and felt refreshed as I entered my car. I pulled out my phone to reactivate the GPS but before I did, I thought this would be a great moment to browse my emails, since this was in the middle of the day. Perhaps an interested client was waiting in my inbox. My heart pittered a bit. I noticed an email from a new partner company I was planning on working with as we had decided to co-run a retreat together in Virginia. I quickly opened the email, expecting it to be an update on their excitement in working with us, but then I read the words:

We have decided to no longer work with Project Passport.

What? No, this can't be happening. I read the words over and over. Oh, and it was happening. I immediately felt sick to my stomach. I had never felt so sick in my life from an email. Rewind back to a couple of weeks earlier. I had worked diligently to bring this partnership together: creating contracts, crunching numbers, presenting the plan, working on the website, organizing hotel reservations, and the whole nine yards. This had to be a joke! How could they do this to me? I had given so much time and care to this new endeavor, yet they were throwing my company away like a piece of trash. They had not even bothered to call me! What hurt worse was that I had built a personal friendship with this team, all of them. This was like a slap in the face and a punch in the gut. I sat in my car deflated and on the verge of tears. How did such a pleasant day just turn completely dark in one quick second?

I quickly scanned the rest of the email to learn they did not want to participate in helping us find clients to join the retreat. They wanted us to organize, co-host, and find clients for the retreat while they merely received payment for their time leading a portion of it. Project Passport was a new company, and they knew this. It was insane for them to think we had that type of influence on our own yet. This was the point of the partnership, all hands on deck. When I got home, I felt frantic. I was not sure what to do. Should I call them? Should I wait for them to call me? I paced around my apartment and quickly babbled the story to my partner, Taylor. He was really upset for me. My hands shook as I desperately texted my mentor asking for an appointment. She wasn't available. Crap. I had to do this on my own. What do I do? What should I say? I can't do this!

After a few moments of my wild thoughts, I felt the calm kick in. Though I was nervous, I quickly typed an email explaining how I was not sure what triggered the change, but I believed this was a partnership effort and that I had hoped we would all support each other in the process. I apologized that this could not have been worked out in a better way with communication and wished them the best. The email was not angry. It was not sad and desperate. It was graceful, and it was respectful. Though my hands were still slightly shaking, I sent it and my confidence began to root within. I did not deserve this, but I was going to get through this.

I prayed to God the next day asking him to help me determine how to move forward. He would not judge me, and I was afraid to tell the team the terrible news. It almost made me feel like I had to admit I failed them. What if I had failed the partnership and it was my fault for the situation? After praying about it, I knew what I had to do. I called an emergency team meeting. God gave me the courage to tell my entire team what had happened. I took a deep breath in and told them how the client pulled out. I waited for the disappointed faces and for the sighs. They never came. Something else amazing came of it.

In the emergency team meeting, I gave everyone the ability to provide their insights and thoughts on how we could proceed from the unexpected outcomes. It was like God's warmth was in every team member because they were all so gracious and encouraging. Each of them lit up like lightbulbs with ideas. We hastily were able to create an action plan to cancel the retreat to the public and to remove it from the website without looking like a disorganized company. We quickly cleaned up and pivoted operations to the next plan. They brought about ideas I had not even thought of. As a CEO, you think you are supposed to have all the ideas, but do not underestimate the power of your team's ideas.

ele

Both of the stories I told you could have resulted in complete despair and chaos. However, they both ended in empowerment and hope. The common thread I know to be true is the presence of God as my closest confidant. Even when my faith was not as stable as it should have been, I was willing to give Him the ability to hear about my dilemmas. I was willing to say my woes aloud and admit I did not know what to do about them. To my amazement, this was enough for God. He helped me find out strengths in me I did not know I had. I was able to realize that my talents and those of my team could translate across a computer screen because we went virtual. I was able to show grace in the face of coldhearted rejection from people I trusted.

These situations are not unique in business. They are very common because life is always changing, along with our circumstances. It does not matter what is happening because there is one thing that does not change in your situation regardless of how crazy it all gets: God. If you gave Him your heart, then He has signed up to be your business and life partner forever. If you do not give Him the ability to work with you in business, then you will have to face those situations on your own. I can promise you right now, it probably will not end well. He helps you manage the instability of emotions to help you make sound decisions, since as we both know, decisions can be life-altering. He provides a voice of hope and reason that translates through those who you can trust around you.

One of the best parts about having God as your business partner is having a rooted confidence in your decisions. When you know you have prayed and asked for guidance in your decision making, it takes away the pressures of making the wrong choice. You know you have done the due diligence spiritually to move forward. The habit of asking God starts to become second nature to the point that you will develop an instinct about people and situations that are right or wrong for your company. You must continue to tap into Him over and over in order to work your faith muscle as you grow.

ele

WHAT DOES THIS MEAN FOR YOU?

Allowing God to become your business partner is easier than you think. It just takes some time to step back and re-evaluate your operations and principles to determine why you need to incorporate Him into all future business processes. There are a few areas you need to explore in your business to begin the process of including God. Note: You *do not* have to have a religious company, nor do you have to convert your business into one to do this.

Values. A great place to start is looking at your values and principles as a business. Where did these values come from? Are they based on emotion, money, or impulse? Really explore if you have a set of business values that you have created from your core. Your business values will serve as your Northern star in dealing with situations like partnerships gone bad, pandemics, difficult clients, and so much more. One of the most powerful things that you can do to strengthen your business values is to tie them to biblical principles. When you tie your values to aspects of the Bible, they allow you to root yourself into unwavering truth. The Bible is unchanging; hence, your values will stand strong, and in turn, you can make tough business decisions against a rock-solid set of values based upon God's word.

Ask. You need to invite God into your business. He will not force Himself into places where He is not invited. You have free will although free will can be risky if unguided. Why not have an all-knowing, best-idea-ever, partner on your team? Did I mention, He never takes days off...not even holidays? Pray to God letting him know you want Him to help you with your business. Let Him know you cannot and will not do this alone. There are many entrepreneurs who do it alone but unfortunately, it results in severe outcomes like depression, panic attacks, isolation, and many more factors.

Ask Him Again... and Again. Just because you invite him to help you with your business does not mean you stop there. You must utilize Him constantly in your business processes. From determining pricing to organizing your team to setting up protocols, ask

God to bring you clarity and discernment. I picked people who were not good team members initially, and they hurt more than helped my company. Over time, I learned to spend time praying for team members before I started the interview process asking God for the qualities I needed. He would be right there listening during the interviews helping me discern who to keep and who to deny. Practice asking God for guidance on the little and the big decisions before you do anything else.

Co-Create. When it comes to mentors and team members, you cannot take them in your back pocket everywhere you go. The only team member who can make every single planning session, meeting, brainstorming hour, and decision moment is God. It is important to allow God to work through you as well as alongside you. I asked Him to help me say the right things and write the best words in this book. This co-creation experience is powerful because now you are this human being doing fantastic things with God's power working through you to produce some magnificent outcomes.

Want to know if you are co-creating with God? Have you ever given a speech without looking at the script but somehow gave a message that inspired the crowd? It was like the words just came through you, and you were not sure what you were saying? Have you ever typed a blog and it flowed like butter? Then, when you read it back, you were like, "Who wrote that?!" Those are examples of co-creation moments with God. Those things just do not happen from thin air. Sometimes you could have had these moments not knowing you were co-creating, and that is okay. When you *intentionally* co-create, you are able to tap into this flow whenever you want, and you are empowered to produce an even more dynamic level of content. You reach a higher level of inspiration than ever before. In essence, you do not want to create with God passively because you will miss out on glorious possibilities.

God + Business Tip #6: God as your business partner will take the pressure off your shoulders. You no longer have to depend on your own emotions and thoughts. After inviting God into your business, make it clear what areas you want Him to pay special care in. Of course, He will help you as a whole but there may be parts that are crucial to address. Those areas, you need to be mindful in specifically asking for clear cut guidance for well-organized outcomes. If you are not sure where to ask for help, at least ask for general support over your business and ask Him to reveal the areas that need His help. He will help you pinpoint the leakage.

Save this quote to get you through:

"God is the partner who gets your business project across the finish line, even in the last waking hour."

CHAPTER 7:
PLACING FAITH IN ALL THE RIGHT PLACES

I keep nailing the message of faith into your mind because I wholeheartedly believe it is one of the most powerful tools a human being can ever carry through life. While it is important to have faith in what God can do in the process of our entrepreneurship journey, things can really get confusing when you are in the midst of the experience. There may be moments when you feel desperate for the next transaction because you must make payroll. There may be times where you need a service to pan out because you invested so much money into it. There are so many situations where you are leaning on the hands of man to ensure your business goals are met.

How often are you internally screaming pleas for a client to say yes to your proposal? How often are you crossing your fingers, hoping your team member does a good job at the project you have assigned them? How much do you depend on the money in your business account to determine the total future of your company? We must know business success does not stem from our work alone. It takes people believing in our journey and those customers willing to invest money in our product or services to better their own lives. One of the hardest lessons about business is this: Depending on a man (or woman) or item will disappoint you. It will disappoint you many more times than you can ever count.

STORYTIME

I sat in my car in shock with tears brimming in my eyes. It was already dark and chilly outside, but I took my car out riding to give myself time to sort through my thoughts. 2019 Fall was in the air as I drove my trusty Corolla around the block, not knowing where I was going. The music was off, and it was just me and God. Was I just a terrible leader? It had to be me. We had lost two team members over the span of just a few weeks, and I felt like the entire company ship was sinking. Though my company was less than a year old and we had not gained much traction yet, I thought pulling together a committed team would be a great step.

I had so much hope and faith in these people helping me spread the mission of mental wellness and travel. They felt other things were more important. Regardless of their true reasons for leaving, I felt used and thrown away. I know they did not have bad intentions, but my emotions had gotten the best of me. I had done everything right, so I thought. I hosted a careful interview process and really took my time to get a feel for people. Yet, they still quit.

During the car ride, I called my right-hand girl and first-hire, Hannah, and said to her, *"What if I am just not a good leader?"* She immediately refuted this idea to my relief, reminding me how committed I had been to her and the team. As she continues to do to this day, she talked me off the emotional ledge and got me back to reality. Yes, these people quit. We were not in desperate need to refill these positions. It was not the end of the world, and I had to get my head back into the game. High School Musical style. Yes, I am a fan and yes I am terrible at basketball. I had to pull it together. Wiping the tears from my eyes and turning my attention to God, I told Him how I was doing my best and how I just needed guidance on this journey. *"Sabriya, you can do this,"* I said aloud. My hands gripped the steering wheel tightly as I headed back home.

ele

ANOTHER STORYTIME

And the rejection rang in my ears like a resounding bell to the nation, *"No one wants your stupid company services, Sabriya."* Those words were the negative ones Satan wanted me to hear. Oh yes, I heard them loud and clear. Fast forward to winter 2020, we were finally breaking into the wellness retreat world with a virtual twist. In fact, we were on fire yet just that quickly, the fire extinguished as we were rejected not once but three times by three different clients in the same week! To make matters worse, they had all received handcrafted proposals which took hours to complete, and one company even took part in a sample retreat demo.

I was devastated. So much rejection in one week made me sick to my stomach and to my soul. My head was spinning. I was wrong. Everything about me was wrong. Everything about Project Passport was wrong too. Each of the rejections were along the lines of the fact that our services just were not exactly what the client was looking for. I felt stupid. Perhaps they were reminding me of the truth after all: We just were not cut out for this type of work, and we needed to abandon ship and go home.

I had so much hope in these clients because we were really working hard as a company to hit the month's deadlines. I felt like we had let these clients down, and in turn, now our company was being let down financially. In order to learn a bit more about the reason why the clients did not choose to work with me, I decided to send them each an email asking them where we missed the mark on our services.

Miraculously, each of them said something along the same lines. They were looking for more of a casual, entertaining experience, rather than mental wellness and personal development. I was completely in shock. For days, I was digging this dark emotional hole only to find out the clients did not have a problem with our services. The services were simply a mismatch to their team's preferences. We literally did not offer what they were asking for, and it was not our fault. We weren't losers after all. My downward spiral, averted!

Happy dancing erupted in my heart as I felt the shower of relief appear not too far behind. I decided to turn to God again in prayer and this time, I prayed a bit differently.

Both stories that I shared with you had a single trend. I had placed my faith in human beings, and I failed to place it where it should have resided—God. So much woe and sadness because I had high hopes that people would act a certain way to benefit my company, yet I did not realize how it was a losing battle. My allegiances belonged to the Lord. God reminded me that I should never have faith in what man (or woman) can do for me but what He can do *through* man for me. You can never place your hopes in a human soul, but you can place your hopes in the creator of all souls. God can place messages on the hearts of people for your good. Ever seen stories where people did something amazing to save or help the life of another human and the interviewer asks: *"What prompted you to do this?"* Sometimes the person who did the great act responds with: *"I am not sure, I just felt like it was the right thing to do in my heart."* This may have happened to you at some points in your life, as you may have gone above and beyond for people in a way you did not expect to do. Someone was praying, and God elected you to be a part of their solution.

When you place your hope in the souls of individual people then you leave your outcomes to chance. Emotions are fickle and people are constantly changing their minds. To hope someone will give you what you want knowing the instability of the human mind is a recipe for disaster. God is unchanging and decisive. When He has something for you, He will make any arrangements necessary to make sure it happens. This is by any means necessary. This means He is willing to reach even the most anti-God people to persuade them to support the missions of those who do have faith in Him. No soul can avoid His touch, even the not so nice ones. Ever had someone who was typically not good to you have a change of heart? God had your back and that person had no choice but to abide. God is going to make it work for you regardless of who He has to go through to do it!

When I finally understood this concept of having faith in God over humankind, the relief was completely overwhelming. God had already placed this dream in my heart, and there was no way He was going to allow a team member or client to rule the outcomes of this company. In addition, if I believed in God, then I had to understand that people quitting or choosing not to use our services was a perfect part of the plan. What if I had kept a team member who was going to steal from me in the future or who was going to quit during a time when I really needed them most? What if I worked with a client who had a totally different expectation of our service and then hated working with us because we were, in fact, not a good fit? I had to understand that God knows clients and team members better than I ever will. As I mentioned before, His plan and ideas are usually 1000% better than our own, hence, we must learn to trust the outcomes.

Sure enough, weeks later, we received fantastic clients who needed our specific services, and we were able to hire a more dynamic and exciting team with a better sense of comradery. Your best team members and clients want to work with you, but if you block them out with faith in the wrong things, you will find yourself hitting a brick wall repeatedly. There is no one client, employee, business loan, or opportunity that deserves your faith more than God.

What about money? How do I focus on God if I need these people to pay me? I knew you would ask, and I have the same response to you. You cannot have faith in the dollar amount in your bank account. If God created the opportunity or dream, He will provide the resources for you to fulfill them. This does not mean you sit back and do nothing. You must continue to actively work towards the goals as you uncover the surprises and breakthroughs along the way. However, do not be disillusioned, He has your clients lined up and ready to work with you when the time is right.

If you must work a part-time job for a little bit of capital, do it with vigor. If you must pitch to hundreds of investors because it is the route you want, do it and do it well. Remember, God will pick the right investor for you if you ask Him. If you must cut down on your spending significantly to stay afloat, then downsize and embrace the process. Faith in money itself is not the answer because you could have the money and completely blow it. You must have faith in God providing the avenue for financial opportunities, and you must have faith He will show you how to use those resources in the right way. Having faith in money alone is a situation waiting to leave you heartbroken with dried up funds.

What about the law of attraction and faith in the universe stuff people talk about? Is this it? The universe and attraction is God. God works through the universe and the world to help you navigate your way to His will. He cleared a path and provided a plan to Moses, Noah, Jesus, Esther, Ruth, and every person who has ever trusted Him with all their heart. This does not mean you will not come across difficult roads. The universe theory alone leaves life to chance. With God, you are a warrior and the odds are forever in your favor. God equips those who have faith in Him, so they are prepared for the difficult moments, and He reminds you constantly that your victory has already been won. The universe cannot promise you those things alone because the universe changes and well... it is frankly unpredictable.

God will constantly challenge you on where you decide to place your faith. He wants to help you, however you must allow Him to help you. I remember when it was time to start trusting my team members to lead retreats without me, and I was terrified. After a few days of agony, I realized I was dishonoring my faith in God by depending on them alone to do a great job. I took a step back and asked God to put the right words on their lips and for Him to give me the right words and methods to properly train them. The solace it brought me was beyond freeing. Of course, they did great, and it worked out. However, had I placed my fears on my team and made them feel inadequate, I would have been creating a recipe for disaster. God helps build, not destroy. You run the risk of destroying what God is trying to build for you when you place your faith in the wrong places.

Let me make one thing clear. People will continue to disappoint you when you make the faith switch, but the disappointment will not impact you in the same way as it did before. You will function from a place of realizing that it was just not for you whether you like it or not. I am not saying you will not be hurt if you really wanted something to pan out and it did not, however, you will see this occurrence as a hurdle that does not stop the whole show. You hurt, you cry, and you recover in order to discover the areas and people that God has activated to support you in your growth.

WHAT DOES THIS MEAN FOR YOU?

You understand why it is important to place your faith in the right place, but there is a process to get you there. You have a world where everyone is telling you to place faith in everything else but God, therefore, it can be quite an overwhelming journey. You must first understand what prayers to utilize when you are trying to make the transition of faith into God and not humans or items. These prayers should be your new style of praying from now on. Of course, you do not have to say the below prayers verbatim, as they simply provide a place to start. Feel free to modify as needed for the prayer to make sense based on what you are asking.

1. When it comes to needing something to work out with a person, I usually say: *God I ask that you touch the heart of {insert person's name} to help {insert what you need here}. I know I cannot have faith in his/her actions alone, and I must believe in what you can do through them to help me live your will. I ask you to help them see {insert benefits you want them to see}. If this opportunity is not for me, I understand Lord, as I know you will always provide me with what is best. Amen.*

2. When it comes to needing an item, place, or thing, I usually say: *God I ask that you work through {insert item, place, or thing} to show me I am on the right track. Please help me manage my decisions associated with {insert item, place, or thing} and help me remember to keep my focus on you most importantly. Amen.*

The main takeaway is that the prayers alone are not based on the world but on what God can do through the world for you. It is easy to set your eyes on the wrong prize when you start praying for the wrong things. Remember in my previous chapter where I explained the danger of praying for things that are not of God. There is no need to be in fear as God adores us. This verse reminds me of just how special each one of us are to him: *"And even the very hairs of your head are all numbered. So do not be afraid; you are worth more than many sparrows"* (Luke 12:7).

No one is trying to keep you from praying for what you want and how you want. Just know what God wants for you is a million times better, and the satisfaction you will receive from doing it His way is literally out of this world. I have lived it, and I know it.

The second step to help keep yourself focused on placing faith where it is due is to: assess yourself. There are going to be times that you get anxious or overwhelmed in business. Think about the source of that frustration. Ask yourself if you are upset because a person will not act how you want them to act. *Are they not buying even though you have worked with them for weeks? Are they not showing up to your event even though they promised?* Whatever it is, you must determine if you have misplaced your faith in man instead of God. If it is in God, then you know the outcome is the right one, whether the person reacts in the way you want them to or not. If your faith is in the person, you are going to beat yourself up or stress over the outcome because you feel that you did not do enough or you were not enough. That is not a safe space to reside.

God + Business Tip #7: When you place your faith in God, outcomes do not become so personal. You understand they are circumstantial occurrences that are necessary on your path towards your goals. Remember, the only thing that is solid and unbending towards your success is God. When the God card is in play, there is nothing the enemy or indecisive people can do about it. God will have the final say.

Save this quote to get you through:

"To have faith only in the world is to give up your life. To have faith in God is to gain a whole world." (based on the original Bible verse)

ele

WHAT'S NEXT?

Many dark things arise in business because you are exposed to many people, situations, and experiences along the way. You become much more open to mental health struggles, your existing fears are elevated, and you become hyper aware of yourself more than ever before. As everyone says, "Business is not for the faint of heart." I take it further by adding, it is not for a heart without God if you want to thrive in business.

There is so much that you will have to manage in regards to people, money, and problem-solving scenarios, and these require abundant wisdom—a wisdom that can stand the test of time and provide you with a guiding set of principles to follow. God has provided the wisdom you need through the Bible as a resource and through direct connection with Him. I constantly believe I am the luckiest business owner in the world because I have God on my leadership team. There are many people who choose to lead without Him, and the dark trenches seem to cut them in a much deeper way. Fortunately, God has empowered us to step on the wrath of Satan and all of his negativity to combat the difficulties of managing a business. Now it is time to face the dark parts, together. We have got this. Let's... jump! Oh, did I mention I am a little afraid of the dark? Flashlights, please.

PART III: THE DARK TRENCHES

Business can create a hell on earth
for those without armor.

CHAPTER 8:
NO ONE THING CAN MAKE OR BREAK YOU

Feedback can be hard to accept. We are often raised to believe that negative feedback is bad and that we should do anything we can to avoid triggering this type of feedback. It just is not fun to receive when it is bad. The uneasy feeling in our stomach is enough to make us want to stay small and run from our dreams at the sake of avoiding negative opinions. The crazy thing is, we are human, and we are always at risk for negative feedback. Jesus came to be the Savior of our world, and people still crucified Him! He received the worst feedback of all time because it resulted in His death at no fault of His own. People hated Him that much and hated His ideas so profusely that they were willing to torture Him and end His life—brutally.

Now understand, Jesus did nothing wrong, and people still did not like Him. You can do everything with the purest of heart and intentions, and people will still find a reason to feel as though you wronged them, or you have a wrong opinion. You can have the best product with the most positive reviews around it, and someone will find something they dislike about it. That is part of life, and it is a huge part of business. When they killed Jesus, they thought they broke Him, and it was over. You and I both know how the story ends (or you will now): He rose from the dead! He came back bigger and better on His way to Heaven with the Holy Father. The same power Jesus was given to not be broken by those who hated Him is the same power you have been given to overcome what negative things people can say about you and your business.

Had Jesus decided the negative feedback was too much, He could have made a quick call to God and said: *"Look, I know you sent me here to save the people, but I just can't do it. I know you have given me purpose, but I am just not going to use it."* Now had He said that... I do not want to even imagine what the course of history would have looked like. Imagine a world where you are never forgiven for anything you have done wrong, and your life is completely based on your wrongdoings. This was the risk of what could have happened had Jesus succumbed to the haters of His word.

What focus area is your company or non-profit in right now? What if you allow all the clients who did not like you to have their way by shutting down or quitting? What would happen to all the clients who loved you and the ones who still need you? If they do not receive your product or service, what emotional or physical pain are they at risk of feeling? My point is, there are high stakes here. You have a mission that is far-reaching and greater than you can even fathom. Your decision to give up based on feedback is bound to cause a domino reaction. The people you touch can touch other people who touch other people, and the impact goes on. Imagine if you are no longer a part of that ripple. What if people do not get to that impact they need in time? What if you were the one standing there with "hope" on a silver platter for this person, but you disappeared because your naysayers told you to go.

ele

STORYTIME

I stared at the phone hazy-eyed and emotional. I was so embarrassed. I had just gone through the reviews of all my most recent retreats. While an overwhelming amount of them were amazing, in fact, raving, I could not help but notice the bad ones. Some spoke of how they did not like me calling their name randomly during the retreat sessions. I had just wanted to include and engage them. Some pointed out they thought I was pushy for adhering to a topic they wanted me to skip (although that is what their company paid for). One person felt that the tools we provided were things they had already heard. *Oh gosh, did everyone feel that way on the retreat?* I felt horrible.

My first big contract company retreat had a few very unhappy campers (more than I expected), and I was in complete shock. I had been waiting for this delayed feedback from the coordinator. I had done many retreats since the very first one, but when it finally came, all I could think was: "Oh no, all my retreats must have sucked if the first company did not love me!" Had I known this feedback earlier, maybe I would have stopped while I was ahead...if I was ever ahead. While I know I was thinking illogically, I felt extremely insecure and like a failure. *Maybe I am just not cut out for this. I need to let it go and find a new thing. What were you thinking in the first place?* My brain was running a million miles per minute.

Later that afternoon, I called a good friend and business project partner and she responded to my struggles with words that changed my life. Jennifer said to me: *"Sabriya, no one business can make or break you. Not one business made you. Not one business will break you, girl."* I sharply inhaled for a moment and blinked tears back. She was completely right. It took a series of experiences to build the beautiful services my company brings to the table. There is not one client who gets to decide how my company turns out, no matter what they say!

If I gave up on what I was doing because of negative feedback, I could not have a hand in helping people rethink suicide, discover hope, find purpose, rekindle faith, explore inspiration, and rebuild goals. What about the impact that these people could make in turn for others? If I allowed one or two entities to break the cord of my operation, I risk breaking the cords of hundreds or possibly even thousands of people. That is the bigger tragedy, much more than a few unhappy reviews.

ele

When God took the time to carefully craft the business model that I would bring to the world, He knew everyone would not like it. My personality was going to be too much for some people. In fact, I had one client review that thought my bubbly personality was an act! They thought I was faking on the retreat. How mortifying is that when little do they know I am the goofiest and most whimsical person in the room most days? Not in a bragging way but in a– this is really who I am kind of way! Anyone who knows me, knows I am outgoing and I laugh way too much. Yet people are going to say what they assume. I share this to say, people will think they know you and judge you, even when they know nothing about you.

With my business, our services were not always going to be the best fit for everyone. Our perspectives and opinions will not always be appreciated. People are not going to agree with the way we go about our mission and people won't like our motto. However, when God developed this vision in my mind, God was not worried about naysayers. He was worried about me staying focused on the mission to change the lives of others by impacting their mental health. Unbeknownst to me, there was already a built-in shield put in place to protect my company from anyone who tried to tarnish the heart in what we do. You have the shield too. Grab it!

If God has something for you, no one can make or break it. It doesn't matter who they are, nor how big they are. He is the only one who has the power to change your company's direction and best believe, if he does change it, it is going to be for the better. He never promised us bad things would not happen. He simply stated He would protect His people and what they bring to the table. Yet, we often allow the power of one or two negative pieces of feedback to outweigh the feedback of many.

One point to mention: Feedback that is less than desirable does not always have to be a bad thing. It can be healthy if it is relevant to the growth of your company. Some feedback can be just what you need to get fired up and provide an even better product or service. You will never be able to satisfy everyone, however people who truly give you constructive feedback can help inspire you to take your company up a notch. They may provide feedback which helps you make your processes easier and improves your client experience. God does not want us to be ignorant to areas we can improve upon. If we refuse to grow and think we know everything, we will fall behind in business, and we will not find success.

In addition to dealing with negative feedback, business is going to magnify some of your biggest insecurities. Okay, a lot of them actually. The feedback can, at times, make your insecurities worse. Satan is going to love it, too, because he is going to get the chance to whisper them into your ear every chance he gets. In business you may be in the most vulnerable state you have ever experienced in your career. You are hoping people will buy from you and trust you. Your worth can feel tied into every service or product you provide. Everything you were insecure about in life before will only become more heightened in business. If you do not like your voice, you are probably going to dread talking to clients on calls. If you are not a good writer, you are going to be terrified to send emails. If you are not very creative, you are going to cringe while designing flyers. Those negative thoughts are going to bombard you like an avalanche. You are sensitive because you believe everything you do will impact the success of your business.

This is normal. But... you will not feel this way forever.

Where God resides, Satan cannot. If you allow yourself to trust God through those insecurities, you will realize they do not make you. There may be areas you are not as strong in, but He will place people in your life to help fill in those gaps. For example, I know my attention to detail is poor. I always have a typo somewhere or I may forget to include things in emails. I am the person who always forgets the email attachment being referenced. I was able to hire highly detailed people to ensure those mistakes were avoided. While initially I was insecure about this quality I carry, I realized what makes me a great business owner is the ability to see the big picture without getting bogged down by all the details. I am willing to start a new project or service understanding it will not be perfect in the beginning. I can admit I do not have great attention to detail to my team and they know to review my work extra hard.

If you do not work through your insecurities with God and through possibly seeking coaching or counseling, they will hurt your business. You will hold back, and you will not function from your highest potential. You will make decisions out of fear and limitation, not strength and empowerment. Satan will gladly help you stay as small as possible so you cannot live out the will of God. In addition, when you receive feedback, there is a high chance you will crumble because it will heighten and exacerbate your insecurities. Be willing to admit to God where you feel you are struggling. He already knows what you are afraid of, and He has a plan.

ele

WHAT DOES THIS MEAN FOR YOU?

Feedback is crucial in helping you direct your business effectively. While you do not want to pivot for the needs of every single client, you should consider negative feedback when it comes your way. However, you must create a filter for this feedback to ensure it is something actually relevant to your growth.

The best way to determine if constructive feedback is worth implementing is to ask yourself a question: *Do I feel worse with this information or does it make me think more about how I can do better on things?* God has given you the gift of intuition in your heart. You know if someone is just a nasty client who is having a bad day versus if they are providing feedback with some sustenance. I have had conversations with people who left me feeling terrible. I chose not to move forward with their feedback, and I do not regret it. I have received feedback from people who have inspired me. I decided to make those changes. Your gut knows when something makes sense for you and your business.

Another way to determine if the feedback is worth implementing is to ask yourself: *Do I continue to receive similar feedback along those lines?* This is a tell-tale sign you might want to update your business process. People are not conspiring everywhere to ruin your company. If you have clients from different transactions providing similar feedback, then it is worth exploring.

The final way to determine if feedback is worth it and probably the most important way: *Ask God!* Tap into God about what you are feeling. I have had people suggest that I implement different programs in my company. I have sought God's guidance and as I prayed to Him, my heart felt heavy. This let me know the direction I was considering was not bringing me life. The thought of implementing their ideas made me feel disconnected and less than authentic. God does not make you feel either of those. When your emotions start dipping into the ground, you know that feedback is not aligned with God's constructive feedback for you. When you trust what God puts on your heart about how you should handle feedback, you will be surprised at what He will do to confirm it for you. You will see signs of how you either dodged a bullet or made the right changes.

Nonetheless, as I mentioned before, there is not one person or business entity that will get to decide if you are successful in your field. The only person who gets to decide this is you, and God is your biggest cheerleader. If you give up, then the naysayers win.

God + Business Tip #8: You will never be everything for everyone. God did not give you a gift meant for everyone. Just as animals in the world have a space and a place to impact the ecosystem, you have been assigned a special part to play in the human ecosystem. You do not see a tiger trying to eat flies because this is the job of the frog. Are you letting the negative feedback of naysayers cause you to lose your focus or are they making you want to give up? Check yourself when you read feedback and watch yourself for illogical thoughts.

Save this quote to get you through:

"All feedback is not your feedback. Sometimes it can be the reflection of someone else's mirror."

And the bonus one from my awesome friend, Jennifer Moore, an amazing Christian life coach I mentioned earlier:

"Not one business or client can make or break you."

CHAPTER 9:
DON'T LOOK BACK

"Flee for your lives! Don't look back, and don't stop anywhere in the plain! Flee to the mountains or you will be swept away!" -Genesis 19:17

The Bible story of Lot and his wife escaping the cities of Sodom and Gomorrah is one that I think every young child raised in the church hears at least once. The story is often used as a reminder to listen to God or bad things will happen to you. I see the story much differently. Here's a little recap from my perspective of how everything went down. Time for "Quick Bible Stories 101" from the slightly kooky mind of Sabriya. Here goes:

There were a lot of crazy things happening in the two cities of Sodom and Gomorrah to the dismay of God. People were acting up and acting out. God was appalled at the behaviors and He was over it. He decided that these cities were to exist no more but sent angels down to save select people, which included a man named Lot and his family. These were people God saw worthy of surviving His pending wrath. Lot tried to warn other people to save them too, yet, they did not listen. They kept the party going like tomorrow was promised. God did His thing and the city underwent destruction. As Lot and his family were fleeing the burning cities, one of the angels warned them not to look back. Just imagine Lot, his two daughters and his wife, terrified, running for their lives with hellfire and chaos happening behind them. Lot's wife could not

resist the urge, and she looked back. She clearly didn't
understand the assignment. In the blink of an eye, she
turned into a pillar of salt. Lot's wife was no more. The
rest of the story gets a little complicated, so I will leave
it there.

When I think of the story today, particularly in business,
I think about the struggles that I had when I first
started. I was terrified when I took the leap leaving my
9-5 job behind with only a little bit of savings There
were moments when I was so scared of where I was
running to in this business that I just wanted to make a
beeline and run right back to what I knew. I would flirt
with job listings, keeping them in my head as a "just in
case," and I would even consider working a side gig for
when money started to get a little low. There is nothing
wrong with working and running a business at all, but
in my case, it was a travel business, and it would have
been very difficult for me to balance the two. Besides, I
had been experiencing severe anxiety and depression
in the workforce because I knew it was not the place I
needed to be. In my heart, I believed I was doing the
right thing by running my company, and I had to fully
lean on God. To this day, I still do not regret my choice.

You may be working full-time while starting or running
your business. You may be working part-time. You may
have taken the full leap like me. It does not matter where
you are working from, you must keep moving forward in
the space you have created. Every day you walk into a
new life, and you create a new world, which helps shape
your future. You are going to continue to take big and
small steps away from your old life in order to succeed
in your business. Perhaps, you get to a point where you
are ready to quit your job. Or it is possible you must

relocate. Maybe, you must let some old friends go because they are holding you back. Whatever it is, you must accept the inherent risks and fears of what you are losing and what is to come. Lot and his family knew that staying in the cities was not an option for their survival; the same applies to you. Your purpose cannot survive and thrive in the old life you had.

If you are obsessed with the life you had before, you will deteriorate the future you are creating. You will hold back and not complete things with the fullest level of commitment. Before you know it, you could end up right back where you started because you were just too afraid to keep running forward. When you run back, you cause your dreams to perish. They begin to fizzle and start to turn into a pillar of salt, too. Stop looking back. Don't look back.

There are special windows of time and opportunities that God develops specifically for you; however, if you are not there in time, they will not wait for you. It only gets harder and harder with more time passing, responsibilities, and complications that can arise. Giving birth to your light is not an easy task and you have to be ready for your due date. There is a time and place for everything in life and you can be the biggest hindrance to your purpose if you continuously miss your window.

Now this is not saying to never learn from your experiences. You do not have to turn your head all the way around like Lot's wife and look back, but rather, you can look through a rearview mirror. Remember where you have come from to remind yourself why you are going where you are going. Know what it took to get you where you are even if it is not where you want to be. Don't repeat the same mistakes. Remember what you find relevant from your past life but understand there is not enough room in your suitcases to take it all with you. Just whatever you do, don't look back... or you are going to be really salty about it. Yep, I am truly awkward and I refuse to edit this lame joke out!

ele

STORYTIME

What was I thinking to leave my job when I had no income coming in? Yes, I literally quit my job to start a business with no income sources besides my student refund and a bit of savings. Things started to get tighter and tighter as I approached the end of 2019. I welcomed 2020 feeling entirely out of sorts because I had been without an income for about six months. I seriously started contemplating my whole business. Maybe it was the wrong business. Every doubtful thought flooded my mind. The first retreat packages we sold were not going to net much revenue, and things were looking scary with the pandemic approaching. It was my fault. I had undervalued our packages. Month after month, I scrambled with my depleting bank account, and thankfully, I had the support of my partner to help with our day to day bills. However, I did not want to depend only on him. I wanted to contribute more and I did not want him to bear all of the pressure. I wanted better for us.

With the pandemic looming in 2020, my account got lower than I would have wanted multiple times throughout the early months of the year. This was before our initial burst of virtual success later in the year. In desperation, I reactivated my real estate license and started working with a friend who had become my client. It was terrible. I felt so bad going out to show her homes because I hated it, and all I could think about was my business. Hours of my day I would spend trying to show her homes, and I felt like I was dragging my feet with bricks. After just about one week, I told her I could not do it anymore and eventually deactivated my license. I was reminded that my purpose was ahead, and if I go back, I would only find frustration, no matter how large the check. Isn't it funny that we think money will solve all our problems?

Purpose ignores the norms of society, and it sure does not care what is in your bank account. See what I did there? The title is back full circle! Nonetheless, it is true. Furthermore, God made purpose, so all bets on doing life normal are off when you are following His assigned path for you. He always makes a way.

By the end of 2020, I was able to replenish my bank account and move back into a place of comfort. In addition, to my surprise, I was approved and had received unemployment support as a business owner to help fill in the gaps. Guess paying my taxes all these years meant something for once because, Mr. Government, I needed the help! Things were looking up as I ended the year with more in my business account than I had ever seen since launching my business over one year ago. I had gotten a taste of what looking back could do to me, and I was determined to never allow myself to do that again.

This story is not to convince you to go hungry and quit your whole career. Please do not email me that you had to move to the streets because you left your career to start a business because of this book! When you make big moves and decisions, you cannot take them lightly. When it came to my full-time business move, I had some luxuries in the fact that I had a partner to share the burden of finances. I also knew I could talk to my parents if I was really struggling (though I would never ask). I had options and support systems built in place. However, I did not lean on them, and I stretched every piece of my money and really avoided buying nice things, so I could be independent. I rarely ever went shopping, prepared my meals as often as possible and scaled back on vacations. I sacrificed a lot to maintain the full-time entrepreneur status because I was determined to give my purpose a fighting chance.

Praying for guidance is crucial in this stage when you are not sure if you should go back to what brings you comfort. God may tell you that you did leap too soon, or He may tell you that you are going the wrong way. Either way, do not plan based on your fears and emotions. Explore the entire situation and your resources. Remember the Bible story of The Drowning Man? He ignored all the help who approached him as he drowned, but he kept saying God would save him. He drowned and came to learn that God was sending the people to save him. In essence, he failed to accept God's help by not accepting the resources available to him. Spend time crunching those numbers and tapping into people who can help you make a way in your business. Make sure you investigate every option because it is easy to miss them when you are dwelling on what you had back then.

I cannot tell you what you should or should not do in the next steps of your business. Nonetheless, you must remember to focus on what is in front of you. God will never send you backwards. If He asks you to go back to your job, it is to propel you with a new lesson to learn for your business or a new person to meet. This is where discernment comes in and you must differentiate your own impulses from what God has placed on your heart. If you have high-level responsibilities like children or dependents, you may need to go back to work more hours. Even if that is the case, God will not allow you to do this in vain. Your perspective on the steps you take will bring meaning towards your goals, and you will survive the difficulties. The paths will get jagged and crooked and confusing, yet, God's still voice will rise above the rest – if you let it.

Find what works for you and whatever you do, keep moving forward. There are things that did not serve you back then, and you must flee them. Some parts of your lifestyle were not conducive to your purpose. You know what held you back then. Do not let it hold you back now. You know what will happen if you go back there. God holds your purpose so dearly as he crafted it by hand, moment by moment. Are you willing to risk ruining one of the most beautiful gifts you can ever hold in this life?

WHAT DOES THIS MEAN FOR YOU?

I want you to think about the changes and adjustments you have had to make in order to pursue your business dreams. Now take some time to think about how far you would go to make sure you did not go back to the life you had before.

As a matter of a fact, imagine your life before you had the purpose you live with today. If you have not found your purpose yet, imagine a life before you knew what you were passionate about.

Ask yourself these questions:

• What are the differences between these two lives?

• What are the positives about my purposeful/passionate life? What are the pitfalls?

• Am I willing to give up the business purpose or passions I have for the comfort of what I knew before? Why or why not?

Now, if I am right, you will pick your life of purpose in your business every single time. Even with the pain and sacrifice you have to make personally, you are still willing to walk the path. If you do feel otherwise, I encourage you to re-evaluate your business and if it is the space you truly want to be in. One of the most powerful things you can do for yourself is move on from things that are not working to bring you joy. Do not waste time trying to operate a business that does not feed your purpose and your heart because it takes way too much work. You will want to quit, and you will quit.

Next, make yourself a game plan for the worst-case scenario in regard to your alternatives in business.

First, write down what can go wrong.

Then, write down what you could do to address it.

Finally, explore if this action you are taking would be considered *progressive* or *regressive*. If it is progressive, then you will grow or develop in some way to be better in your business. This action would expand your resources in a positive way where you will feel good about it, and you will be able to continue to do great work. If it is regressive, you will feel terrible about the decision, and you will hold your business back. You will know the answer to the question on impulse when you complete this exercise, so do not hold back.

God + Business Tip #9: Avoid chasing the illusion of happiness in what you know. Happiness is in what you do not know because that is where God dwells. He wants to challenge you to take chances with Him and He wants you to trust the future He has prepared. God does not reside in your old ways, as He is committed to renewing your mind (He says so in the Bible!)

Save this quote to get you through:

"Your destiny lies in everything you don't know."

CHAPTER 10:
A DISTRACTION OR AN OPPORTUNITY

When I first started my business, I was terrified to say "no" to anything. I felt an obligation to jump into every "opportunity" that would get my name out there. I am sure you've experienced or are currently experiencing the same thing. You know any moment can be a turning point for your company, therefore you do not want to miss out. I constantly convinced myself that the one time I said "no" to something, it would be the one thing I needed to get where I was hoping to go, and I would instantly regret it forever. Day in and day out, phone call after phone call, I was convinced I was the hardest working entrepreneur there ever was. I participated on any podcast I could get my voice on and joined any "connection" phone call I could take.

The wear and tear started to kick in. Imagine running on a treadmill at the highest speed, and no matter how fast you run, somehow you only make it one mile, yet you feel like you have been running for hours. You are out of breath and you know you have been working our tail off however, for some reason, the results are just not showing on the external end. We do the same thing with our lives, as we constantly find ourselves going and going with no goal in sight. We think we have done everything right just to end up with nothing but a mirage. A bonafide desert mirage.

Satan is the king of mirages. You think you just came across the biggest opportunity of your life, and before you know it, everything is spiraling out of control because this "opportunity" was in fact a distraction. It was not the opportunity you had been looking for. In business, you are going to constantly be challenged with people pulling you in all directions. The more you grow, the more everyone wants a piece of the pie of your success. Even when you are not considered "successful" by your own standards, the "perception" of your success may still float under the noses of others. They will invite you to collaborate, partner, connect, pick your brain, learn about you, etc. Satan will use well-meaning people to suck you dry mentally and emotionally until you have nothing left to give. You can either blindly run the treadmill or choose to be observant. You can either keep reaching for the mirage or you can start praying for discernment.

ele

STORYTIME

I was furious. I felt so used once again. I was duped as usual. Another two hours of my life in which I can no longer get back. I had done this to myself repeatedly. I thought I would be able to avoid it this round. This was about the tenth time I had gotten on a seemingly innocent call where someone wanted to learn more about me and my business from a "collaborative angle," and then it turned into a free "pick-my-brain" session. The feeling of guilt and shame would wash over me like icy water because I would waste my day on phone calls with people who only seemed to take and take from me. I was supposed to be taking the time to lead this company to better places. The only place we were headed was back to square one. How could I be so gullible?

These people did not realize, or maybe they just did not care, that they were abusing my time. Deep down, I know it was not their responsibility to realize it. It was mine. If I could not respect my own time, then of course, they were not going to respect it either. I knew something had to change or I was going to keep chasing my tail. I knew I needed to do better, but I didn't, however, one moment did it for me. This moment was what made me decide to never let my time be held hostage by the people around me again. The distractions were no longer going to trick me. I was done.

It was a warm, summer day, still living 2020 pandemic life, and I was so excited because I was being connected on a call with a big-name company in the wellness industry. No, I won't name names but know they are mainstream. I just could not wait for this call. My heart was on the moon and I know this could be my moment. I had been waiting for it to come for days and my hands shook as the phone rang. The lady answered the phone, and my voice trembled slightly as I confirmed I was speaking to the right person. My awkward laugh almost derailed me before I pulled it together and got professional.

The call was a whirlwind– sharing a bit about my company and learning a bit about hers. However, the mood changed when she began to ask me questions about how I have been getting my clients and how I get myself out there. Something felt weird in my spirit as the questions seemed to really be edging on how my company worked in detail, like the details holding your secrets to your product's specific success formula. They were a huge company, so why were they asking about how my small business was getting clients in our shared industry? This lady from this big-name company did not seem interested in collaborating one bit no matter how hard I tried to move in that direction. She never was. When I got off the phone, I felt defeated. I felt empty. I felt used and disregarded. It was the final reminder that my spark was not for everyone to get for free, and I had something of value that I needed to focus on. These "collaboration calls" were not it!

I began to pray to God to please help me discern opportunities from distractions. I asked that He would not allow me to get lost in everything going on and all of the "opportunities." I prayed He would help me keep my eye on the prize no matter what came my way. Just because things were shiny, I knew they were not always mine to grab. God truly answered my prayers. There have been so many times where I found myself swaying into lanes where I didn't belong, and God would remind me where I was supposed to be. Countless times people will share opportunities for me to pay to be a part of their programs to "help" my business or offer for me to join their events. I say "yes" when it makes sense and "no" when it does not. There is a root in me growing deeply to the ground, and it keeps me stable in what I believe in, not what others believe for me.

The beautiful essence of "no" changed my life. I began to pray hard for discernment when opportunities came and if they were not in alignment, I could kindly turn them down without the guilt or fear of offending. While everyone tells you how important it is to say "no," you should think of it as saving your time and energy for the right "yes."

ele

There is something sweet about knowing God has specially packaged your dreams and opportunities for you. You do not have to walk around in your business feeling stressed about all the things you could be doing. When we act like everything is supposed to be for us, it is almost selfish. We are choosing to grab every present under the Christmas tree, even the ones that are not our own. Now we have a home full of stuff, with wasted space and time to go along with it. Opportunities can, especially ones that are not yours to have, damage your business. We are taught all opportunities are good, but this is not true. Every opportunity is not created equal because some are decoys Satan planted to keep you from reaching your highest potential.

Think about those people you know who have twenty business ideas, and they are running five companies, yet none of them are doing well. That person may be you. Do not feel bad. Be aware of what you are doing to yourself. Jumping onto every idea may not be the way to go for your true purpose. I have those friends who every time I call them, they have a totally new business and plan trashing the one before. It hurts to watch them on this hamster wheel spending thousands of dollars and hours trying to do multiple things without really getting any substantive results. Of course, I give my two cents, but we must be careful in friendship preservation 101. Satan wants us running all over town with a million ideas because it will keep us from the core ones God created specifically for who we are meant to be. *Sometimes more is actually less. And less is more.*

There are also those business owners who get stumped all over for their time and money through these "so-called" partnership opportunities. This may be you and this is no longer okay. In business, everyone wants to partner with you, but not everyone has the privilege to do so. Some people are hoping to jumpstart their business off yours. If this is the case, you must be fully aware and consenting. Some people may want to steal from your business, ideas, and followers, and it can happen right under your very eyes. Satan may appear to be the nicest person who seems to pose the "perfect" partnership with no strings or risks. Always, remember to check business contracts, especially the fine print. I learned the lesson, and I learned it well by not having my documents in order. In business, there are no real rules, hence all the cards are on the table; if you do not have God sitting with you in the game, you do not have a fighting chance.

What about those "golden handcuffs" as opportunities?

People sitting in jobs they hate for years because of big salaries and promotions are living the life of what they call, "golden handcuffs." Satan likes to compensate you, and he will do so gladly. Satan has endless money pockets due to his dominion on Earth, therefore he is happy to fill yours– if you let him. Do not get it twisted, Satan can bring people success in this world but there is always a catch. This doesn't mean someone should quit their job in the name of starting a business right now, but it is to warn you that when it is time to take the leap, you can miss the mark for years. If you are already in business, do not worry; He has a plan for you too. Satan can keep you small by making you think there is only one way to succeed, even if what you are doing is not working. You may need to pivot and make changes to get where you need to go, but Satan has you thinking there is only one way. Bottom line, he can make you static with beautiful distractions keeping your life practically on pause. Your mind is in a trance of "opportunities" that no longer exist in your plan.

Okay, what if I go to a conference or masterclass to get out of my rut?

Finally, conference and masterclass events are an available option, and I recommend you do not attend with the mindset that these events will be your savior. They are helpful tools, but they can deplete you of valuable time and money. So many "zombie entrepreneurs" attend one masterclass after the next, hoping to discover the golden key to success, yet they have been carrying it in their back pocket all along. These workshops and events can seem like they are opportunities, but when you attend, you may feel more insecure, empty, and confused. And your pockets are a lot lighter. You gain a new tool here or there, then realize the tool does not fit your business like you thought it would. It is important to take care in selecting these events to attend by having a clear intention on why you are attending and what specific goals you will achieve because of your attendance.

Cue elevator music. Waiting. Feels like the dreaded holds when you call the airlines during a busy time of year. Waiting… for… the… next… moment.

Waiting is a natural part of the opportunity process.

Some opportunities may look appealing, yet God tells us to wait, which requires patience. *"Be still before the Lord and wait patiently for Him* (Psalm 37:7)." He asks you to "be still" not to allow opportunities to bypass you but to hand-deliver you the opportunities He has picked for you. And trust me, the ones He chose far exceed the ones you may have had in mind. This has been clear to me time and time again. To be clear, no one is telling you to sit and do nothing. Sometimes you will make mistakes like I did, wasting time in business. God knows you will fall, and He is always there to help you recalibrate. You must want it. You must want what He has in mind for you, even if you do not always know what it is.

ele

WHAT DOES THIS MEAN FOR YOU?

You may be thinking: *"This sounds much easier said than done. I am not supposed to accept all opportunities? How will my business make it then?"*

You have the tools! Grab your bag of faith and your hands of prayer. They are all you need to comb through the jungle of opportunities. Knock away the snacks and scare away the lions! You are almost reaching the treasure you seek. You are Indiana Jones in your own right! Prayer is key because it allows you to reshape the reality ahead of you.

I roughly use the following prayer to help me gain clarity on whether things are opportunities or not:

"God please direct me to the right way to go in business. Please grant me discernment so I know what is really for me and what is not. Please reveal anyone who should or should not be in my path. Amen."

Remember, you break down the prayer how you want. You develop your own relationship with God; therefore, you can ask Him in your own style. Here is a quick action guide for when you are in the dilemma of determining if something is a distraction or opportunity. Practice the following acronym:

W - Withdraw yourself from the situation to think. Refrain from jumping into a quick response. Tell the person you will get back to them. Save the invite in your email until you are ready to make a choice. Do not begin the application just yet.

A - Ask God to give you guidance and discernment. Pray your heart out. Allow yourself as much time as possible to seek Him, and keep an eye out for internal and external signals to help you with your decision as they come.

I - Investigate your feelings. What does your inner spirit tell you? Something immediately went off in your inner spirit about the "opportunity" when you received it. What did it say? What emotions arose? Dread, excitement, fear? Over time, watch how your spirit processes the situation.

T - Track what you gain from the "opportunity" versus not taking it on. Is the cost for the outcome too great? Consider what is at play. Your time? Money? Both? At some points, you may realize the numbers really do not add up, and you must be honest with yourself.

This W.A.I.T. acronym can be your go-to in your decision-making process when determining if something is meant to help you or distract you. There have been times I accepted free gigs because I realized the opportunity was worth my time. I needed the valuable experience, or the exposure would bring me clients. There were situations where it worked out, and I am glad I did it. At other times, I wish I could have gotten the time back. Either way, I learned from both situations greatly, and I get better every day. I am now at a point where I comfortably direct people to my rates when they want to "pick my brain," and I do not waste time trying to attend every event. I offer pro bono advice when I see fit and I charge when I want. I realize the assets I need are inside me and I know they are inside of you too.

God + Business Tip #10: Just because it was thrown your way does not mean you were supposed to catch it. Stop taking every plate placed in front of you. Some food should be left uneaten and you can feel good about it. Business is less about speed and more about stamina. When you get to those forks in the road, do not hesitate to turn to God for direction. Trust yourself to own the path you take even if you miss the mark. You can always get back on track, and most important of all, learn from those mishaps with God by your side.

Save this quote to get you through:

"Every opportunity is not your opportunity."

CHAPTER 11:
WELCOME TO CHAOS, SATAN'S PLAYGROUND

At first, I could not understand why my life would be amazing at times, and then suddenly, it would turn into a pure mess. I look back at journal entries from my first year of business, and I was in complete disarray. One journal entry detailed how excited I was and how everything was going to be okay, while the next one talked about how much I was failing and how the world was falling apart. I could not understand how my life could go from good to bad so quickly. It was not until I started to notice my emotional patterns that I discovered the source of my turmoil. Two "innocent" little faces would peek from behind my shoulder, and they would combine to create a super demon called chaos. Before I knew it, I was on Satan's playground of bad choices, I was the star. Tearing down everything in my path, even if it meant sharp words to those I love and hateful words to myself.

I used to get nervous when I did not have to spend much time putting together my virtual retreat experiences. People would tell me how it took them months and days to prepare whole speeches and presentations with many hours of rehearsal. I did not have to do all of that, and it terrified me. I would pray to God the days before my retreats for the right words to cross my lips and the right activities to come to my heart. Of course, I had an overview of what I planned to do, but I allowed myself to fill in the gaps during the experience rather than planning before.

Satan is funny like that. Even when you have a blessing, somehow, he tries to convince you of how crazy you are. He wants you to feel like you are completely out of your mind for having talents and abilities different from those around you. It becomes isolating and may make you feel like an oddball. Before you know it, you are trying harder to hide your gifts behind the way you believe you should act. You begin to fall into line of being like everybody else, losing your unique talent along the way. You do not want to be too loud. You refuse to be too bold. You must keep quiet because you can't go against the grain. You can't have it all figured out.

A terrifying place to live is hiding behind yourself. Satan wants so desperately for your mind to run like wild with thoughts of fear, insecurity, and confusion. He loves the confusion most because then you do not know where to turn. Your friends--anxiety and sadness—begin to run around and around laughing in your face. I know the feelings all too well. I remember the moments where I felt the emotional hurricane whipping my face, and I tried to envision the road ahead, but it just would not come into focus. I was readily trying to readjust my business to look the part. Yet, it was a part that was not me. If this truth sounds familiar to you, you are not alone.

God will *never* give you the spirit of confusion. Never will He make you feel stressed for being confused. Satan is the curator behind those emotions because he loves to play with your heart and emotions. While it is normal for humans to experience a difficult decision-making process, we can acknowledge that the choices are hard while still functioning from a clear mind of strength. Confusion is the absence of a decision-making process. If you ever feel confused about a business decision, ask yourself if this has been triggered by outside forces. Most times, someone planted an idea or thought in your head, and it has begun to take root. In turn, if you are not careful, this root can intertwine with your thoughts causing the confusion to arise. Maybe someone recommended you change a key feature to how you run things causing you to second-guess your own plans. Or you could have run across a competitor's social media account, and you are now convinced you are running your business all wrong.

～ elle ～

STORYTIME

That one girl asked for gift certificates. I should add them to our website and take three to four hours to design them.

Hmm... veterans need help too? People tell me all the time. I will make a retreat for them, even though I have no idea what I am doing.

Should I become this "woo woo" holistic wellness guru of the universe? Yes, it is where the industry is going and people seem to like this, so let's start using the weird wellness terms on the website and in my videos because this looks about right. Quick note, there is nothing wrong with the woo woo gurus but they are not me.

I should work with this company because someone recommended it. Maybe I need to do the partnership, even though it is not exactly in line with what I am trying to do here.

These statements were toxic self-talk throughout the earlier part of my entrepreneurship journey that stemmed from the ideas of others. I tried and failed at every single one of them. I remember the utter failure I felt each time. Each time, I realized that I allowed confusion to make my decisions. I did not seek the guidance of God, and I got exactly what I asked for, a mess. It had gotten so rough on me that I became scared to make business decisions. I began to lose trust in myself. *Maybe I was not fit to run the business on my own.* Those well-meaning suggestions floating through my life were the most harmful daggers to my confidence. Satan knew just how to place these ideas because they tapped into already existing insecurities. My insecurities were as follows:

I need to provide everything a client asks for, even if I do not offer it. If I do not, they will think I am incompetent and not like me or the company.

I should help every population I can, even if I do not have much expertise in that area. If I don't, I am not good enough, and I am not a good person.

If I do not look the holistic wellness guru part, I might as well give up in the industry. Besides, people do not look like me in the wellness space. No one will like me for me. Even if it means I lose myself, I will fix this.

I may not be smart enough to know what is best for me so I am willing to work with people who may not make a good partner organization for me.

These are the negative thoughts I have carried with me in business. Fortunately, through prayer and consistent communion with God, I am reminded of my capabilities. This is not to say it is always easy, however I choose not to carry the burdens of my insecurities alone. God strengthens me with excitement and ideas, despite the whirlwind of the world's expectations around me. I decided I would bring any decisions to Him, rather than living in my own mind of confusion. I know alone, my flesh is bound to react from fear and insecurity, but through God, I react through strength.

ele

By inviting confusion into your decisions, you allow it to guide your outcomes and they are never pretty. What are you willing to do to keep confusion at bay and lead with courage? You may not know which way to turn in the exact moment, but you must expect that God will provide you the guidance you need (assuming you seek it). Satan does not always come in an angry tirade. In fact, he may be wrapped in a pretty bow. Those well-meaning people who seem to have your best interests at heart may really have your best interests at *their heart*. However, I challenge you to ask yourself what your own best interest of heart is.

Everything goes wrong at once in business sometimes. The hurricane will come, but you can decide to stand solid or spin around with it. People are going to quit the same week you have a huge event planned for your company (this happened to me). You may receive a rejection email right before you are to speak in front of people (this happened to me too). You may question why you started your business in the first place (happens to me every now and again). You may get into an argument with a loved one right before an important business meeting and you must keep a smile on your face (this definitely has happened to me). Life does not work around you. It works through you. You get to decide if you want to become a part of the chaos or let the chaos answer to you.

There is a Bible story that I always heard in church, and it is such a funny one to me. It is the story of when Jesus was on the boat with his disciples and a storm hit. They were hanging out and doing fine at first but when this storm hit, they were like (well in so many words): *"Wait. Whoa, Jesus we are scared! Umm, help! This is not okay."* Jesus is napping peacefully on the boat while the storm rages on and the disciples are panicking. Finally, Jesus casually tells the storm to *"Quiet! Be still"* (Mark 4:39), and I could imagine His facial expression towards the disciples. He looks at them like: *"I have made miracles, walked on water, healed people, and you all are crying over a storm? You have got to be kidding me!"* I mean I would have felt silly as a disciple knowing I am with the Almighty Jesus, yet I am still scared of a storm. Jesus asks them if they have any faith, and the disciples apparently had forgotten they were with the real Jesus Christ as they start to whisper amongst themselves asking who the man is.

This story makes me giggle because it is probably how God feels about us constantly. He works these miracles for us, but as soon as some chaos breaks out, we act like we do not even know who or what is happening. God already told us He had us covered, but it is like living with amnesia because we forget when Satan brings his circus to town. The chaos of the storm is imminent; however, the outcomes do not have to end with you cowering down in fear. Find the eye of the storm. Find your quiet place with God and it is the best way to annoy Satan.

Have you seen any scary movies lately? One of the movies that I saw a while back was the movie, IT—the one with the terrifying clown who ruins lives with some scary stuff. I am not going to lie as some parts still traumatize me to this day. The last segment of the multi-part movie series shows the adults, who were once terrified by IT the clown as kids, finally destroy him once and for all. Spoiler Alert—at the end, the kids end up telling IT how he was a sellout, loser, and how they were no longer afraid of him. They talked mess to him letting him know how much of a punk he is. How amazing was it to watch this creepy as heck clown shrivel when he realized no one was afraid of him anymore, which made him less powerful. Besides scaring the life out of me, the movie ended up teaching me a bigger lesson than I had ever expected.

Evil and chaos feeds off fear. The more fearful you are, the more chaotic your decisions and the scarier your life. Satan loves it when you are afraid because it allows him to turn up the heat of stress in your day to day. Fear is the culprit to chaos. Think about how many ridiculous things people have done over the course of history in the name of fear. There is a long list of stupid wars, battles, and murders. Fear essentially makes us dumb and I have been dumb a lot because of it!

When I am afraid sometimes, I literally yell this loudly in a room: *"Satan, you are a loser, and you always lose! You do not get to win this one, not now, not ever!"* I remind him how much he will not get to feed off fear and despair in my life. I let him know that there is no room for him in my story. It is the one time in life I feel so great about making someone angry. God gives you the superpower of mental strength, even with tough odds in front of you. Do not let Satan take this away.

"Fear" and "Confusion" are best friends and are the innocent faces I mentioned earlier in the chapter. You do not want to join them and make it a trio because when you do, pure chaos ensues. Satan is the master of tricks and games. While his circus may seem harmless, it morphs into this monster, gnashing and ripping at everything in your life piece-by-piece. While there are times you will feel nervous about your decisions or you may question the way to go, you must remember that God frames your choices as opportunities. Something beautiful can be created from any of the choices. God wants you to trust that He will keep you on the path you need to follow, windy roads and all.

ella

WHAT DOES THIS MEAN FOR YOU?

Fear and confusion are a nasty concoction because they feed off one another. People fear what they don't understand. Many did not understand Jesus was the son of God, and they were evil to him because they were confused and afraid. What a terrible way to react to the Man who calls the shots in your life.

You must do the internal work to start addressing what fear and confusion look like in your life. Remember,

Satan is sneaky, and he will help fear creep up on you like a leopard, and before you know it, you are crashing down mentally and emotionally. First things first, you must acknowledge the indicators of these two animals:

1. What does confusion look like for you? How do you know when you are starting to spiral on that back-and-forth train?

For example, when I am confused, I get very stressed out all day and feel flustered. Even the smallest tasks begin to take everything out of me. I exhaust easily and become short with people around me. I start refusing to make decisions, even simple ones. I get really crabby, almost like any angry baby I admit.

2. What are the signs of the presence of fear in your life? What happens to your mood and your demeanor? How are your choices impacted through the lens of fear?

For example, one way that I personally respond to fear is anger. I get frustrated, and it likely pours onto people who are trying to help me. I get mad at my circumstances, and I get mad I am facing such a difficult situation. I become a runner and I kick in my flight response at a moment's notice. I do not want to deal, therefore I escape.

Once you can call out the reactions, emotions, and signs of the two experiences, you are able to then start mitigating through them.

1. When you hear the sirens of *confusion* going off in your mind, ask yourself the following:

   • Must I decide at this moment?

- What is the source of this confusion? In other words, did someone/something trigger it?
- Is staying in the place of confusion easier than making a choice?
- How can I make the transition of placing this decision in God's hands, so I do not have to go at it alone?

2. When you hear the sirens of *fear* going off in your mind, prepare yourself:

- Call yourself out for functioning from a place of fear.
- Call Satan out letting him know he has been discovered. His cover has been breached.
- Determine if your fear has been coupled with the dangerous culprit of confusion.
- Ask God to help you gain the courage to manage the threat of fear.

Fear and confusion do best when they are undetected and when you let them fester. They are like weeds. They start to form under the soil of your life taking root deep, and suddenly, they rise from the ground. Goodbye peace, hello chaos. You are doing all you can to yank those weeds out, but oh how they are rooted deep. You prevent the spiral by trusting God and your abilities to see this situation through... and the next one too.

God + Business Tip #11: If you are not self-aware of your experiences in business, you will not be able to perform at your highest potential. One of the most vulnerable, yet effective things you can do is to own your fear and confusion. At times, you need to admit to your team you are conflicted on a decision, and you need time to process. They will appreciate this more rather than you making a chaotic decision. Sometimes you need to tell someone you are scared to receive the empowerment you need.

Save this quote to get you through:

"The fearful and confused set themselves up to lose."

CHAPTER 12:
LOVE, DEATH, AND PURPOSE

Purpose is not as elusive as people may make it seem. Everyone is on a purpose expedition and some may even pay gurus thousands of dollars just to help them find it. There is nothing wrong with seeking support on the journey to become the greater you but how much faith are people placing in their guru to find purpose? To expect another human being to locate what only you can find is risky business to me. You are setting yourself up to be disappointed and likely a bit frustrated. You are ninety-nine percent responsible for doing the work to find the beautiful tapestry of a life plan already residing in your soul. Coaches and gurus can help you poke at it by asking you the right questions and exploring the right things, however, you must be the one to call it what it is.

Love births purpose. Or perhaps, it is the other way around, and purpose births love.

I think they both happen in firing succession over and over in your life back and forth. You are not going to always love the work that purpose takes, and purpose is not always going to squeeze out things you love. However, when you decide to take the journey with God in the front seat beside you, you will find joy in the dichotomy. You will have a late night working on a project related to your purpose and feel overwhelmed, but the joy and peace in knowing God has crafted this path for you will bring you solace. People are not being honest when they say they love everything about their purpose and what they do. They paint a false picture, which may cause you to panic when you realize you do not feel the same way all of the time. God knows things will get hard and you will have less than ideal moments. He longs for us to never give up because He always has something special in store.

Purpose is an adventure. You will skin your knees. It will have highs and some wild lows yet this is what makes the process all worth it. No matter how hard you fight, purpose will come for you even if you are kicking and screaming. Either you slay the beautiful beast or you learn to walk with it in grace. Either way, purpose does not care what you have going on. It wants to be all up in your business and as I mentioned before, it surely does not care what resources you have.

ege

STORYTIME

The nights were filled with tossing and turning. It was early 2020. I had finally regained some traction in my business as the pandemic hit, but something still did not feel right. I was out of focus and my purpose felt blurry. The self-doubt was kicking in, as I was not making much money with the small women's retreats that I was hosting at the time. I was finding them terribly hard to fill with clients every other grueling week. I felt defeated and considered shelving the business altogether until the end of the pandemic.

One night, I found myself somewhere in a beautiful, open field. I do not remember the landscape, but I remember it being calm, serene, and stunning. My focus, however, was mainly on the woman standing in front of me. She was beautifully dressed in all dark colors, and she had this peaceful aura about her. I knew in my heart that she was the Angel of Death. She needed no introduction. My mind immediately went to fear, but that fear did not translate to my body. I felt eerily fine. Just fine. The conversation was serious, as she asked me:

"Do you want to stay, or do you want to go?"

I stumbled for a moment but regained my words. *"You mean like go... go with you?"*

She nodded.

Me being my goofy self, I responded, *"If I go with you, will I at least go to Heaven?"* I even let out a chuckle, but I was half-heartedly serious. I mean, I hoped I would be on the list. I definitely did not plan to go to Hell, and if this was the case, I preferred to remain on earth to have more time to get myself right. You feel me? Haha, this has me dying laughing when I think about it now but hey, I had to do my due diligence.

To my surprise, she said: *"Yes, it looks like you are thus far, but you do have more things you have left to do here. It is up to you."*

I let out a little cheer inside. *I am going to Heeeeaven! Woohoo! I made the cut!* Then, I took another moment to ponder. I do not know what came over me but I slowly said, *"Yes, I know there is more left to do here. I guess, I guess, I will stay."* I felt a bit of reluctance in my voice. What if I squandered my chance for Heaven if

I stayed here on earth too long? This might have been my best chance to make it. What if I messed it up later?

Even with the doubts, something told me I made the right choice. She was gone before I knew it, and I woke up more perplexed than I had ever been from a dream. I even told my partner, Taylor, the next day how I had the oddest dream about the Angel of Death approaching me. The dream sat with me for days, as I was not sure if it was something that really happened to me or maybe it was just my unconscious mind. Had I said yes, *would I have died right there in my sleep?* I could only wonder. Well, I did not die, which was for the best, I am sure. Then again, I wondered if maybe I had in fact left my body, and it happened in real life. The dream felt so real, and the impression on me was strong. Anything was possible at this point.

This story gets even more intense as a few weeks before this dream had occurred, I had a random friend whom I did not know too well recommend a Christian book to me called, *When God Steps In, Miracles Happen* by Neale Walsch via Facebook messenger. When he first sent it, I was being cheap and did not want to buy it because it cost a little bit more than what I was used to. For some reason, I kept feeling this urge and before I knew it, I was checking out with the book on Amazon. It happened so fast, almost as if I was possessed by the spirit of Amazon spending. I mean come on. Amazon makes it way too easy to buy stuff online. You are telling me all I have to do is swipe right and I already paid? That is a recipe for disaster, well unless you bought this book on there, teehee!

Back to my friend. The book ended up being a collection of several stories and accounts of people from all over the world who had miracle encounters with the spiritual world of God, Jesus, and Angels. I had picked up the book a few times and read a couple of stories a day. It had been a week or two since I had read another chapter, therefore, I thought I would spend my prayer morning reading a chapter. I tried to pray most mornings and this book had served as a cool source of inspiration. I had been committed to praying and communion with God for about 10-15 minutes at least. This resulted in a successful, relaxing day each time I started this way. I read a quick chapter and started to end my reading for the day, however, I felt the need to keep reading into a second chapter.

The next chapter was about a woman who had experienced a difficult childbirth and her baby was in the intensive care unit hanging onto a thread of life. The woman had a difficult time with God because she was in so much grief and questioned living. She started writing a letter to God, and later, she laid down in a hospital bed. Suddenly, she felt a terrible pain in her body and passed out, only to be approached by... wait for it... the same woman who approached me in my dream just a few short weeks ago! She even described the woman similarly to what I believe I saw. To my complete amazement, the Angel of Death asked the woman in grief the same question she asked me, whether she wanted to stay or go. The woman talked back and forth with the Angel of Death to determine that she had more purpose in this life, and it was confirmed her baby would, in fact, survive. Fortunately, the baby healed, and the woman was able to stay on earth to find and to live her purpose.

My blood ran cold. My heart raced. I felt my hands shaking as I placed the book onto the table and ran into the room to tell Taylor. His eyes widened, and he was not even sure what to say. I could not believe it. The confirmation was clear. The dream I had was not a dream after all. I realized I had experienced a brush with death, and this was a second chance and reminder for me to keep going and live out the purpose God had assigned to me. I still think about the experience, and in times where things start to get hard, I remind myself of the decision I made to stay.

ele

It does not take near death experiences or dreams to snap you into purpose. They can help but you can start being purposeful right now. You can start by praying to God to help reveal areas in your life where you should be and to remove parts of your life that are keeping you from them. Seeking Him is always the first step in purpose because you are turning to a source of truth and light. When you look for purpose in the wrong places—like other people, social media, television, etc., you will get the wrong answers. You will find yourself on a long, wild goose chase, and you will not win this one.

Purpose takes patience. Sometimes you may not be ready to step into your purpose just yet. God may see areas of growth you need to attain. You may be trying to run when you need to take a moment to walk. Your purpose might be so big that God does not want to overwhelm you by throwing you into it too soon. Rest assured; your diligence will pay off as you continue to do the best you can in the meantime, as your purpose organizes itself. Once it is in your face, you cannot ignore it. God will not let you ignore your purpose. The conviction of *"I need to do this"* will hit you so strong, it will cause you to rethink everything in your life. As I mentioned earlier, you cannot afford to neglect purpose as it begins to take shape into your life because it will starve inside of you if you do.

ele

STORYTIME AGAIN

I was in my Belize apartment in the early days of Project Passport in 2019. I had just started using the LinkedIn platform again because I wanted to get my business out there as much as possible. I saw a message flash across my LinkedIn chat. I was a bit startled because frankly, I rarely received messages. I felt like a nobody on there, hence I was delighted someone was reaching out to me. I thought, *"What do they want with little ole' Sabriya?"* Tickled, I eagerly clicked the icon to access the messenger program. The name of the person looked familiar, but I could not be sure. I opened the chat and immediately my stomach tightened. I felt sick. I felt dizzy.

The words across the chat said: **Edwin passed away.**

I read the words repeatedly trying to determine why the phrase did not make sense. Well for one, I had talked to him recently via text message. Two, he was as fit as a fiddle. The man worked out far more than anyone I knew. He would wake up super early and jog two miles before work each day. Three, he was the most hardheaded, tough mentor I'd ever had, and I appreciated him for it. Now it took time for me to appreciate it, but I did. People like him just do not just die like that. They couldn't, could they?

I rapidly responded trying to understand if the person who messaged me was talking about the same Edwin I knew. I knew who the guy was, but something in me wanted to believe it was a mistake. I realized the person chatting with me was an old coworker from a past internship at an animal health company who worked alongside Edwin and I. As it turns out, Edwin had been diagnosed with a random type of leukemia and passed away within a few months of being diagnosed. How does this happen?

Not the Edwin that took me to this random hole-in-the-wall barbeque joint with his crew of workers on lunch break where I tried my first real barbeque meal. Not the Edwin who would talk to me about his 401k plan and how he had life planned out for when he retired. He never got to retire. He never got to truly bloom the life he was meant to bloom. Do not get me wrong; he had a beautiful and amazing family, but I know he did not reach some of the achievements he desperately desired, personally. He was such a talented person who stayed in a position of comfort in his career, and for that reason, he urged me, throughout my entire two-month internship, to *"Think big."* He would tell me to do and be better than he was. He saw this smart, talented woman in me; one I really kept shoved in a corner. He saw my zest for life and my ability to make things happen. At first, I thought he was too pushy, and I had no idea what he really meant. I assumed he was just being dramatic as he always was, but no, this tough, opinionated man was right.

I could not afford to go through life passively. I could do and create anything I wanted. He admitted to me he had settled and did not go after many of the purposeful opportunities he wanted to pursue. He felt it was too late in his life, but I could still have the chance in mine. It took me losing my mentor and friend to understand the gravity of his words. To this day, I credit him with some of the push it took to launch my business. His spirit reminded me that I could not settle into what I knew. It reminded me this was my chance to chase purpose in life, and I could not afford to waste the blessing God was affording me. Even though he can no longer pursue purpose in this life, I actively pursue it honoring him in the process because his words of encouragement never left my soul. I did not get to attend his funeral because I was not due to fly back for a few more days, however, I am glad I got to remember him how he was.

I was going to go full force, and no one could stop me. Not now, not ever.

ele

Many people die with some purpose still living in their hearts. They do not get to pour out every ounce due to various circumstances. I stand on the brink of death daily; in fact, we all do. We walk around like another day is promised but death is just a door knock away. Or a dream away. I choose to live for those who cannot live their purpose any longer. I will use their remaining ounces left to the best of my ability. When the Angel of Death returns to visit me, and one day comes to visit you, we need to be able to leave this earth in confidence that we did what it took to reside here. Those words, *"Well done, good and faithful servant,"* from God are what I want to ring across our ears.

Your business, your baby, your craft is bleeding with purpose in the most beautiful way. The light that bleeds from it can almost be blinding to those around you because they feel this immense need to gravitate your way. People are attracted to other people who are living in their purpose. Purpose combined with the light of God creates a complete equation for nothing but success in your future. You cannot lose, no matter how hard things get. When you fall, look to Him and He will grab your hand. He will provide a motor to your spirit, and it cannot die down, ever. Some days, your purpose will keep you up into the wee hours of the morning tapping away at the keys, or some days it will have you working on the days you were supposed to be off.

You must not burn the motor of purpose until it makes you sick. Take the days of rest and take the days of work. Take the days of play and take the days of deep project focus. God rested when he was busy building this world, so do not think that you can keep going without rest because it is like telling yourself you can outdo Him. Your purpose never needs rest, but your human body does, and it is connected to your soul as you occupy it on this earth.

God is love. God makes purpose. Therefore, purpose is love. You can manifest the love of God in the world when you live your purpose. What a beautiful and amazing gift to have. This gift of purpose is one of a kind and God made it out of pure love for you.

This business you are dreaming of or currently running cannot be an accident. Something jumped into your spirit. Something kept you thinking hard about it. Something made you believe that it was possible. That something is God, and He is waiting for you to open the gift He has delicately wrapped for you.

ele

WHAT DOES THIS MEAN FOR YOU?

How close do you think you are to your life's purpose? Does it coincide with the business you are starting or the one you already started? Are you starting a business solely for the wrong reasons? Do you have a true heart for the work you do or plan to do? You know the truth of how you feel, and you know the answers to those questions. Are you willing to admit your truth?

When I work with clients in the realm of purpose, I highly encourage them to tap into their values. Take some time to write down core values that define who you are. Narrow down to one or two of those values. Those values are highly significant to who you are in the world and how you interact with people and how you interact with yourself. Whether your value is faith, empathy, love, or family, it is one of the keys to the greater meaning in your life.

Do not take the values to be simplistic. They are so much more. Values run much deeper than you think. Just because you choose faith as a value does not mean you must automatically have to become a preacher. Maybe you help others find faith in themselves, then they can be confident enough to take a chance in life. Through that newfound faith in their abilities and renewed hope, they can begin to discover God who has been waiting for them all along. God often manifests through you in your purpose; therefore, you do not have to traditionally preach (unless you are called to do so) to people for them to experience His love. Or it could be that you value the family unit so much that you are willing to work to help keep families together in the work you do. You could value love so much that you work with young girls who grew up without love in a world of sex trafficking. Your values are flexible and far-reaching. They paint a picture of purpose, and you must be willing to explore the picture with care.

Another key factor in discovering purpose is being open to failure. As I said earlier, purpose is not always pretty. It is messy, and it is stressful at times. It can keep you up at night, and it can nestle into your thoughts all day. With the love of God, comes attacks from Satan. Satan can sense when God is doing something amazing for you through your purpose, and he wants to slap this down as soon as possible. He will plant anxiety into your spirit if you let him. He will paint fear on your heart if you allow it. You must know the attacks are coming in order to be mentally prepared to continue trekking forward. If your business is truly the purpose God assigned you, Satan can never take that away from you. The only way he has access into your life is through your willful allowance of him into your mind and soul. He does not show up looking evil and gory. He is a smiling face, a potential hire, a "nice" mentor, a knocking "opportunity," and without discernment, he can be easy to miss.

God + Business Tip #12: Be mindful of how you treat your purpose. It was a gift delivered directly through the love of God. When you choose to toss it into the corner or to unwrap it with haste, you can damage what is inside. Allow purpose to unravel in your life every single day because it grows and permeates your soul. Your business must lie in the bedrock of purpose on top of the foundation of faith. Without purpose in business, you find unbearable strife when times get hard.

Save this quote to get you through:

"A purpose assigned by God cannot be broken by anything nor anyone."

ele

WHAT'S NEXT?

I am so happy you decided to round the corner on this journey with me. My journey as an entrepreneur has not been easy, but I can say with peace that it was the one of best choices I have made in my entire life, thus far. It has shown me the power of God in a way I had never seen before. I have had some dark moments along the path, but God keeps taking me higher and higher on this journey allowing me to get to know Him and what He is capable of doing through my life. My stories and my words have inspired countless hearts, and this moves me to tears. I cry because I know I did not do this alone. I did not know I was worthy of God using me. I did not know God even wanted me to do what I do for the world. This book has poured from my fingers more quickly than I can imagine, and as I have prayed for God to give me the right stories to tell. I hope they have inspired you too.

God knows who you are, more than you will ever know. Keep yourself in check along the entrepreneurial and life journey. With the bumps discussed in the prior sections, this coming section will bring you home and remind you where you are going. I am obsessed with loving my journey, rather than focusing on the destination. You spend far too much time on the journey to only wait for a momentary victory. Celebrate them all!

PART IV: A JOURNEY THAT NEVER ENDS

And you must pick yourself up from the mud
and keep trudging on.

CHAPTER 13:

FRANKLY, IT'S NOT ABOUT YOU

There are tons of reasons to start businesses and projects. There are even more reasons not to start them but something in your heart and soul told you it was time and you had to do this no matter what the risks may be. With every moment, every win, and every loss too, everything stems back to the day it all began. As you reflect back on the turning point of your business birth, I want to share a bit on mine. Storytime!

~ell~

STORYTIME

When I first launched my company, I was really excited about the opportunity to help others live life with hope and joy, but I was also looking forward to traveling. I always had a heart to see the world, and I was amazed that I had created such a fun business model that stemmed from travel. As you know, the pandemic changed this for me, and I did not get to take my first trip through my company. Had I decided to give up and close Project Passport because I could not travel, it would have been one of the most selfish choices I could ever make.

By deciding to go virtual, we served hundreds of people in a short period of time. We provided hope to countless numbers of people because of the domino effect of the nature of our work. We transformed company teams and changed the hearts of women to be confident and fearless. Though this was not our first choice of how to run as a company, we realized that we had a job to do. We had the responsibility of effecting change in this world. Mental health was tumbling to all-time lows, and we were there to help stop the cascades of people who needed it most. If I had decided to cry in a corner for the rest of 2020 because we could not go to Kenya, I would have never been able to lead our team to a path of even greater success with mental wellness at the forefront of our services. No longer were we centered on traveling, but we were focused on saving lives and spreading light.

It took being in business just over a year and failure after failure to understand just how much my business was not about me. As a matter of a fact, none of the popular social media posts, podcast appearances, accolades, or rewards meant anything to God. While in the worldly sense, I would get excited about them, God showed me that I had people to serve, and I had work to do. The rewards and recognition were just a byproduct of me following His directions. For the first half of my time in business, I was convinced that if some of my social media posts went viral, everything would get better, and I would find success. I also thought the bigger the team, the better my company would turn out. It felt good to run a team of more than ten people. Looking back, I realized this to be a mistake in my thought process. My priorities were all wrong.

The most success I experienced was when I had the lowest levels of "likes" on my social media posts and no one saw me. We were bringing in client after client, however, if you looked on the outside, you would have no idea. Most people think businesses without fame and likes are not doing much but inside, we were seeing growth and revenue we had never seen before. You cannot judge a business by its posts!

This humble success is exactly how God works. He is not in the spotlight flailing you around like a show. He is working carefully and meticulously behind the scenes to help you better serve those who need you most. He is not worried about how the world perceives it. To adopt the mentality of serving your clients and demonstrating God's works through your own body is what our business is all about. You can be rolling in prosperity in your business while not a soul knows and this is the point. God did not put you here to remind everyone how successful you are; you are here to do the work with excellence and care.

The team I had built fell apart quickly. As fast as I put it together is about as fast as it fell apart. I was doing it all wrong. I thought this team was about growing the company as rapidly as possible. The more hands on deck, the more revenue there was to be made. This thought process was completely unhealthy. Little did I know, every single time I brought someone onto the team, I brought a new level of responsibility onto myself. Just as we are the flock who Jesus cares for, as a leader, when you build a team, you are creating your own flock to care for. Huge kudos to Jesus because the whole world is His flock. I had a flock of less than fifteen people, and I was failing them big time. Rather than focusing on caring for and shielding the flock as I should have, I just announced sales goals and told them to keep working.

I am not saying I was not a loving leader because I was. I took it too far, and I coddled my team. I did not give them the space to grow. Whenever they needed help on a task, I practically did the task for them. I rarely invoked any boundaries or discipline. When you don't encourage the sheep to walk on their own and escort them away from danger, they will perish. I was killing my team by trying to be liked and failing to truly create an environment of self-development. I thank God, I had mentors to call me out on these leadership behaviors because I had become selfish and controlling by being a nice leader.

ele

STORYTIME AGAIN!

I sat on the phone in disbelief as my mentor, Lore, explained that if I continued to treat my team members as if they could not do anything for themselves, I would fail them. I was convinced I was one of the best leaders there ever was. I was kind, empathetic, understanding and I knew I was nothing like some of the leaders out there. I was not one of those terrible micromanagers. People should love me as a leader! I was trying to focus on the road as I listened to her on the phone, but my mind was racing. I felt a little embarrassed and nervous. She was the kindest soul, and I knew in my gut that she was right. It annoyed me, still.

I tried to defend my actions by saying, *"Well my team member is not good at this because she says that is her weakness, so that is why I step in and just do it for her. No point in wasting time."* I was into following the old adage: "If you want things done right, you have to do them yourself." Lore firmly replied, *"She will continue to carry this as a weakness if you keep doing what you are doing."* She got me. She was right. My team would never grow and develop if I held their hands like they were children. I would have a team to "help" the company yet I'd still be working harder because I would become a helicopter mom, looking over their shoulders constantly, doing the work for them. My mom was a helicopter mom growing up. While I loved it, it caused me to become such a baby when things got hard as an adult. To this day, it takes a lot in me not to just run to her when things get hard.

I prayed about my conversation with Lore weeks later. It kept swirling around in my head, and the next time a team member asked me to help with a simple project, I changed my reply. I told them to do what they thought was best and then when they finished, only then should they show it to me, and we would go from there. Everything changed in my business. They began to craft ideas and things that I could never have even imagined or come up with. The impressive nature of their work was utterly overwhelming. Now I know what Jesus meant about teaching a man to fish so he can live for a lifetime. I went from practically handing my team fish to letting them catch their own. It was the most beautiful sight watching them bloom and seeing their potential shine. As I said before, God speaks to you in many ways but one of the most common ones is through people. To this day, my conversation with Lore stuck with me. When I start to get too involved in individual team member roles, I remind myself of what it means to help people authentically develop.

ele

The moral of the story is that controlling people and coddling them is selfish. No matter what angle of kindness it comes from, you are hurting them more than you could ever help. You make it about your own comfort and peace rather than helping them thrive and shine. When your team shines from within, by natural byproduct, your company will too. Jesus cares for us by guiding us to live our best lives. He does not force His hand or coddle you. He lets you fall at times to help you learn important lessons. He lets you cry when you need to let it out. He does it all lovingly because he knows the bigger picture is about your growth and development as a human in this world. As leaders, we must carry the same principles to the teams we serve.

Frankly, it is not about us.

When everything is said and done, this life we live is about how we show up to serve others, including the planet and creatures who inhabit it. In a world where it is trendy to post how much you have donated or what you did to help a homeless person, God gives no care to what you do in public. He cares about who you are to your core on a daily basis, especially in private. He did not give you a team to worry about how good they make you look in public. He did not give you successful transactions so everyone can see how many hundreds of thousands of dollars you made this year. He does not care.

The pandemic revealed many predatory and hurtful business practices that were ruining the lives of customers and employees. These predatory businesses began falling one-by-one, along with their CEOs.

Customers moved their money elsewhere and took their buying power to places that showed they cared about their clients and their staff. Employees stopped taking the maltreatment and were willing to live on unemployment or nothing before going back to jobs where they were not valued. We can no longer create a world where people hide behind dollars while destroying other people's lives in the process.

If you must step on the heads of others to build something, you will eventually find yourself living a life of despair. Greed is one of the seven deadly sins for a reason. It creates a climate of compliance to suffering. With greed, people almost always live empty lives full of things. God did not put you here to help suffering continue. He will take care of you generously if you believe you can help while not taking advantage of others.

God gives you a team to mold and grow to help carry out His will for positively impacting the world. God provides you with clients for you to show them His love and care in the work you do. The money is just a bonus outcome for the work you do. I do not care if you are making mugs or cleaning houses for your business, you can show the love and compassion of God to people in all that you do. In every interaction and in every expression you have with others, you have the opportunity to show God's love.

You must understand that business is not about you. If you think you can go into business for yourself and work only to serve your needs, your business will certainly fall. You may make a lot of money, but you will never truly be happy inside. You will buy things hoping to fill the void daily, and your mental health will not thrive the way it should. Just because you see people out there winning externally does not mean they are winning internally. To own a business is to take responsibility for an issue or missing piece in the world. To own a business is to do what it takes to ease the pain of the issue and to serve at the highest level possible.

There will be long nights. There will be extra work hours. There will be days your needs are put behind the needs of your clients and team members. You will sometimes have to work much more than what you are paid to do. You will miss out on things you want to do to make sure your customers are getting what they need. There could be times where you must decide whether to pay yourself or your team members. I have had those a-plenty. You must be prepared to lean on God and not your own wants and needs. All in all, that's business.

∽∾

WHAT DOES THIS MEAN FOR YOU?

When I let go of the idea that business would bring me money and external success, I opened myself up to a freedom to create solutions and to make a difference. Imagine leading your business, or really your life in general, from a place of hope and genuine orientation towards how you can serve others. How would things change? Would you be living in financial fear and scarcity? Would you find more joy in what you do?

The money will come if you focus on what you can do to serve on the forefront. God has always made it clear *"the last shall be first"* and how He will always take care of his children. As a human being, you have automatically been given the right to accept your position as a child of God. It is not something you have to apply for because it has been offered free of charge. College should be too, yet that is another conversation for another day.

You may have always felt like a person on the sidelines, but when you step into what God has for you, you will take your rightful place on stage. You will not be on stage for the glory of yourself, however, you will be on stage to spread the glory of God's light through you. People will gravitate towards your light. They might not even know or want to know God, but you will be the turning point in their lives. To know the kindness and love of God through you is going to be like a warm, sunny day to people who have lived cold, frigid lives.

Here are a few things you can do to help change the lens of your business:

- Spend time writing down how your clients/customers are transformed by your product or service.

- Ask yourself why you started this business in the first place.

- Think about the protocols you have in place for clients/customers and determine if they are completely inconsiderate of your clients/customers and only consider you.

- Ask yourself what the role of your team members are, if you have any, and determine if their roles are about your ego or genuinely placed.

- Ask yourself if you are doing any work to help your team members self-develop on a greater level or if you have them there to do a job.

- Determine if you are playing helicopter mom/dad on your team and how it may be hurting them.
- Place yourself in the shoes of a client/customer and imagine how it feels to be served by your company.
- Ensure your business practices are ethical and non-predatory, no matter what there is to gain.
- If you are providing donated products, services, or funds to non-profit organizations, consider the reason for your broadcasting of this to the world (if you are).
- Ask God to use you for His will, as you know it is greater than your own ideas.

Upon exploring these areas, spend time creating actionable steps to transform your business into one who serves the needs of the team and the clients, rather than just you, the leader. You will be surprised to see the upturn your business will take. People will want to work with you despite having access to other services like yours. People will prefer your services or products over others', even if yours may cost more. People will sense the light of God in you, whether they know God or not, and it will be more powerful than even the best products/services in your industry alone.

God + Business Tip #13: While it is completely okay to have desires for your own business success, never let your personal wants outweigh your obligation to serve your team and customers. God will reward those who follow Him by providing them longevity and hope, while those who take selfish paths will not survive the storms. He will help you feel whole when life gets hard because you will have more than just dollars in your pocket as you will also have a fire inside your soul, which cannot be smothered. And that, my friend, is the greatest reward in life.

Save this quote to get you through:

"Being first in line to honor God will always outweigh being first in line to gain the riches of the world."

CHAPTER 14:

THE PROCESS OF THE PROCESS

STORYTIME

My heart was pounding with sheer excitement and joy as I listened to her spoken word video. I had just discovered a gem on my team and had no idea what this woman was capable of. It was during the early fall of 2020 during the pandemic that I decided to hire her, and I really was not sure what to expect. She was transparent about some immensely personal struggles going on in her life, yet she seemed so eager about our mission. She knew I could not pay her much, however, she still wanted to be a part of the work we were doing in some shape or form. While I was worried about how she would manage her life and her new role with us, I took the leap and brought her onto the team.

The first few months were rough because her personal life took a turn for the worse and the pandemic pounded at her family and future. I had never dealt with such difficulties with a team member in such a personal way. She ended up missing several team meetings and was not able to uphold her required work roles. What she was experiencing was pure tragedy, and I felt so helpless in supporting her. We were not in a place to provide pay advances, and I wanted to support her so badly. I prayed about it, and God reminded me to give her a space of peace and love. Of course, the worldly, paranoid side of my brain wanted to keep my distance. I was trying to be the leader the world says I should be, *"Nice but realistic."* I chose to listen to God instead by just being a continued support for this team member, and I prayed for her to overcome her situation. Some days, I even prayed over the phone with her.

It was a couple of weeks later, and she called me with tears of joy. She had been able to successfully win her battle in the courts and retain what was hers. Her and her children were able to keep their place to live. I was one of the first people she called as she thanked me for everything I had done by providing my heart and ear to support her along the way. I was elated, as I shared in her happiness. We both thanked God as we ended the call. I knew the prayers had worked, and I had no idea how much I had been able to support this woman. I learned a huge lesson that day. Failing to provide support just because I do not have the money to do so is a cop-out and excuse. Your time and sheer empathy are assets in times like these.

Months later, I discovered her spoken word talent that she kindly shared with our company, and it blew me away. The pain, passion, and inspiration in her words were some of the most powerful I had ever heard. I could not believe the world did not know her yet. I was determined to build a platform for her through my company. I was determined to help her message of hope reach the masses. She had layers of brokenness and pain that no one understood, and as she opened up to me over time, I saw her flickering spirit and found myself determined to keep it from breaking. Her talents served as a foundation to the mental wellness mission we serve, and I am forever grateful I took a chance on her.

Had I primarily been focused on outcomes and the destination, I would have potentially made the hasty decision to count her out. I am so glad I did not allow the negative thoughts to make my decision, and I let the compassion of God drive my choices. I decided to be present in her journey, even if it was hard.

~ell~

How many times have you said the words, "I will be happy when {fill in the blank} happens?" I think we have become accustomed to outcomes to the point that we ignore everything happening in between. We focus on the starting point and the end point. That's it. To me, that's crazy! We spend more time in the middle of life than we do in the beginning, or the end combined. Nonetheless, we are practically zombies throughout most of our lives because we can care less what the process entails, as we are just wanting it to be done already.

I am not going to pretend I was any better. My journal has documented my process over the years, and a good chunk of it was just filled with complaints. I did not care to even notice the pieces of the process that helped me become the woman I am today. I was so worried about the money I was not making, the people who were not helping, and the rejections I kept getting, that I refused to see any progress. However, had I taken my time to take in the process, I would have noticed the small steps we had been taking towards our goals, and I would have not continued to make some of the same silly mistakes over and over.

I hired aimlessly. I kept staff on the Project Passport journey longer than they should have been because I was too scared to fire them. I didn't really plan out finances for the journey. So when things got weird financially, I panicked. I got lost in the publications and accolades. All I could see was point A and point B. How much do you relate? These choices kept pushing me in circles more and more, causing me to spiral. I had forgotten to fall in love with the: *process of the process.*

The Bible shares many stories where people had to wait years to obtain the outcomes they sought. Some people wanted to have babies. Some wanted freedom. Others wanted financial comfort and so on. Each of these stories shares one thing in common: The journey in between was the most important part of all. Most of the lessons learned were not from the outcomes. The lessons were learned from the mistakes and obstacles along the way as they pursued their goals. God uses their stories not to only provide cautionary tales but to remind you that their journeys were just as important as their outcomes. Some people chose faith along the way, while others chose to give up on God and to take matters into their own hands. Those who chose faith often received more than they asked for and those who chose the latter, often ended up in bigger messes. If you do not believe me, check out the story about Sarah and her baby. Presenting, a quick run down of a popular Bible story from my mind:

Sarah wanted a baby so bad. The lady was getting old and she was getting more and more frustrated by the day. God kept promising he would come through to help her and her husband have the baby but it was not soon enough. She was sick of the process. Instead of focusing on her marriage and growing in other ways personally, she told Abraham to get one of the servants pregnant. What?! I know right; I had the same response. And guess what? He really goes off and gets this chick pregnant! Sarah is happy at first as she begins to raise him. Then at around 90 years old, she does end up finally getting pregnant herself. Now, Sarah ends up mad at the other woman and the child that is not really hers. She gets so mad that she sends them off.

Yes, the whole thing went to crap because Sarah could not focus on the process. She obsessed over the end goal and now a mom and a child ended up on the hurt end.

Time is going to pass between you and your goals. This is not a punishment from God, but it is part of the process of life to prepare you for the outcomes. Sometimes, you may not be prepared to receive the blessings without the process. The process is your preparation. If you had $1,000,000 in clients waiting on you, could you even deliver the quality of service or timeliness of products? What about $100,000,000? Maybe you could if you are a veteran in the business world, but you might not be spiritually and emotionally ready for everything that came with it. If you are a new entrepreneur, then you would have obstacles to overcome spiritually, emotionally, and logistically.

You can be patient and passionate at the same time. You can enjoy the lessons and adventures as they happen on your way to the top. You can be excited about meetings with people in between, even if they do not amount to a huge return. You can be proud of getting in a small local publication, even if no sales come of it. You can be cheering for your first podcast interview even if no one even listens to it. These are the little skills and abilities that continue to improve within you so when the big meetings, publications, and podcasts do come, you handle them with grace and confidence.

I encourage you to learn new hobbies along your journey. Make the journey fun and worthwhile. Meet with interesting people. Walk in the park to take those breathers. Have a beautiful dinner with a loved one. Write down random business ideas as they come to mind. These are all things which make your life's journey worthwhile. You are going to remember these moments far more than you would the big victories. There will be many victories in which to be proud of, but moments with yourself and with those who matter to you most will carry so much love for you. Most importantly, spend quality time with God each and every day. He makes the process of life bearable, even when you believe it is not.

ﻌﻠﻋ

STORYTIME AGAIN, AGAIN

It was Spring 2020 and I had just completed one of my most successful purpose retreats yet. The women were brimming with excitement as they began to discover their true purposes in life through new activities I had designed, alongside my younger brother. A few days earlier, I was on a video call with my brother, James, working together tirelessly to develop more powerful and compelling activities in regards to discovering one's purpose. Though he is several years younger than me, his creative mind and passion is undeniable. He is pretty smart but I don't tell him too much to avoid blowing up that head of his! It was fun having him on the team as a makeshift intern. We would discuss an idea, play it out, and then tweak it back and forth until we could agree on the best execution. The call went on for hours, but I was so grateful to share such an inspirational flow with my own brother. Periodically, we would laugh and poke fun at each other's ideas, but we kept the main goal in the forefront of the conversation. Sure enough, he was key in creating some of the best activities we had ever done with our clients before.

That evening, after the successful women's purpose retreat, I called my brother and told him the immense levels of positive feedback we received, and he began cheering at the top of his lungs on the phone. I was taken aback for a quick second. He was so excited, while I had glazed over the victory thinking how I could get the next event going so I could make real money. I did not take the time to appreciate the journey to this seemingly small victory. I asked him why he was so happy with humor and sheer curiosity. He responded how we had worked so hard making great activities, and he was happy about how it all turned out. His joy reminded me to love the journey I was on, even when the victories did not seem like much in the big scheme of things. This experience would go on to help us in achieving big outcomes in the future, as we helped more clients reconnect to their purpose in work and life.

ele

Okay one more Bible story for the road. This book is winding down. Sad, yes. Exciting, even more, yes! Remember when Moses was taking the Israelites to the

Promised Land? This is one of the most popular Bible stories of all time. Here's how it went:

Moses finally was able to help the Israelites escape the grasps of the Egyptians as they were slaves for centuries, building pyramids for the evil Pharaoh Ramses and his forefathers. Moses' most known quote: "Let my people go," rang for centuries to come. Well, during the trip, the Israelites got tired of it all. They were extremely hungry, tired, and frustrated with no end in sight as they trudged through the wilderness. They spent so much time complaining and frustrated to the point that they almost were willing to go back to being slaves. Instead of focusing on the victory, achieving freedom after centuries, they were upset about their present circumstances. They could not appreciate the whole experience of the process as they moved towards the land of "milk and honey."

At one point, when Moses left to the mountains to receive the Ten Commandments, the Israelites completely lost their minds and started chaos to cope with their circumstances. They were getting drunk, worshipping false idols, and doing everything they had no business doing. God was appalled and furious. He had just helped Moses deliver these people from years and years of horrible treatment, and this was their way of responding to a temporary inconvenience. They caused their journey to the Promised Land to last decades, four to be exact, when it could have taken less than a decade.

Sometimes, we can be the biggest saboteurs of our own journeys. Sometimes, we are Israelites wandering around the wilderness, angry and hungry (or hangry), refusing to hear what God has to say about where we are. We can delay the moments of relief because we are too busy being mad at the process. What if we saw the process as an opportunity to learn and to get better every step of the way? What if the process became an exciting chance to innovate something new?

I reflect back on some of my biggest moments in business, and they are not about our large transactions or fancy publications. I remember fun team meetings learning more about my team. I think of special moments encouraging my brother during one of our business meetings. I am reminded of long phone calls with my first hire and connecting with her life so much that I truly see her as a friend and support system. I giggle at the silly prayers I would make to God in my little apartment closet about how I just needed him to help my company not fall apart in the pandemic. I knew deep down He was not going to let it happen, yet I still cried like I had amnesia about the capabilities of Jesus Christ. My heart smiles thinking about the process of what it has taken to build what we have built. God, me, my family, my mentors, my friends, and my team.

Never will I preach this whole concept of self-made. I know who was leading this car because had God just left me at the wheel, we would have been in a ditch a long time ago. I am grateful for every single bump. The days where no one showed up to my event; the nights where I did not know if I would make payroll; and the times where I lost partnerships. Every single part of the journey led to the moments of today. I truly enjoy what it means to run a business that is totally not about me and about how I can serve God.

I had no idea whatsoever what I was doing when I launched Project Passport. I barely had a business plan or a point of reference. All I had was faith, a prayer, and immense passion for the work I was about to embark upon. You do not have to have the journey figured out. You do not even have to know what you are doing along the way. The biggest asset you will ever carry is appreciating the process of what it takes to get there, wherever "there" is for you.

I challenge you to focus on the journey in life and to take your mind off the destination. It rarely ends up being what you expect it to be anyhow. The whole experience is a process with some high- and low-level checkpoints along the way. Life is like the ocean. The tide is high at times while the tide is low at others. Sometimes the waves are unpredictable and sometimes they are peaceful and kind. Nonetheless, the water keeps on moving and flowing. It continues the process of the process, with no end in sight.

Truthfully, your work has no end in sight. Even though one day, it will end on this earth, you are just living a trial run for the promotion you will have in your next life with God in Heaven. If you are an amazing teacher here on Earth, just imagine training the angels on their missions in Heaven. If you are a great leader here on Earth, just imagine the initiatives you will lead in Heaven. So, if you are going to work, do it in excellence and give it all you've got. And for goodness sakes, you have got to do something that matters to you. And most importantly, you must enjoy the never-ending journey.

WHAT DOES THIS MEAN FOR YOU?

I am not saying the process will always be easy. You may cry along the way. You may be angry, and you may feel like giving up. I just ask you to appreciate the existence of the process because that is all there is. The process is ongoing, and you spend ninety-nine percent of your life in the middle of it. Your business will go through many changes and tweaks during the process as you learn new ways of doing the work you do. Logistically, guidelines will evolve. You will learn lessons on billing and payments. Contracts will be re-written and new ones will be created. These are all components of the process.

There are two components of the "process" to consider:

- Acknowledging the process itself. Give heed to its existence.
- Appreciating the process of the process. Be proud of your part in the journey as it is unfolding and how you are becoming better for it.

Here are some ways to acknowledge you are in the midst of a major process in your business:

- Your business is undergoing rapid changes.
- You are noticing kinks in your business process, and you have to go back to the drawing board.
- A transaction has fallen through, and you are trying to figure out what went wrong.
- You are going through a phase of figuring out why you got started in the first place.
- Your business is dealing with a lot of difficult external impacts.

These all may sound scary, but you will come out of them better as long as you keep your head in the game. You must show up in order to play. God makes it clear several times throughout the Bible that things will get hard, however He also makes it clear He will be there always and forever. Showing up for the transformations your business is undergoing is a key part of being present in the process. Many people are quick to shut down when their business is going wrong because they failed to acknowledge their presence in the process.

Here are some ways to appreciate the process of the process in your business:

- Be willing to tap into resources for support in approaching the obstacles. God will place the proper resources in your life. Don't be the "Drowning Man!"

- Think about the areas you have grown in from previous situations and how you got to where you are now from them.

- Practice gratitude for the solutions you and your team create to deal with issues in business.

- Celebrate your small victories and accomplishments, even when they just feel like a stepping stone.

- Let God know you are aware of where you are (even if it hurts) and how you are thankful it will not be this way forever through Him.

- Take care of yourself, especially when you cannot control the situation. You might as well take the time to breathe and enjoy the weather or your family for a bit when a solution is out of your control. God is working for you. The least you can do is take some time to enjoy yourself. Give yourself permission.

By appreciating the process, you allow your journey to continue where it needs to go rather than trying to force your life to happen at the speed and way you want. You are honoring God by showing Him you trust the process even though it may feel different than what you intended. At times, the process will feel good and at others, the process will feel miserable. This business world is about moving forward even with the weights on your feet. God needs you to walk just a little while longer, even if you are tired. Your Promised Land is waiting for you.

God + Business Tip #14 (the final tip): Respect the journey ahead of you and make it fun along the way. God wants you to love the process because He has carefully crafted it with you in mind. Make time in your business to celebrate each moment and to reflect on the leaps and bounds you have made no matter how big or small. Do not wait for something big to happen for you to be excited about your life.

Save this quote to get you through:

"With God, the process is worth the process."

CHAPTER 15:

SO... GO FLY

As you approach the end of this ride with me, get out of the car! Just kidding but seriously, I want you to know that you have already won. Satan's biggest fear is everything you have read in this book. His fear is that you will be prepared with the armor and shield of God to overcome his attacks. He is terrified you have found hope and faith in your good. He wants to throw doubt, uncertainty, anxiety, and every negative emotion he can on your path. Satan wants you to be afraid of the success to come in your life and to keep you as small as possible.

After reading this, I pray you are more prepared than ever to handle him like a pro but be warned. Do not let this book be the last one you read on faith in business. *I am not a replacement to the Bible.* You must keep your spirit man or woman alive by feeding him or her. Trust me, my spirit woman gets wonky when I get lost in myself without including God in the process. I get afraid and I begin to backpedal. It almost happened when I was writing this book. It has taken me so much longer to publish than it should have been! Yet, I am growing and learning daily just like you.

My grandpa used to tell me that when he was in high school, he used to run track. During his time on the track, he remembered the faster he ran, the more he felt like he could fly. As a little girl, I remember laughing so hard at him thinking, *"Fly granddad? Ha-ha, okay?"* When I was an adult, he described the feeling and the experience to me once again and for the first time, it was like I spoke his language. I knew exactly what he meant. To fly is to have freedom. He felt the highest level of freedom in his spirit when he ran, hence his spirit was probably flying right inside of his chest as he ran. He really was flying.

Freedom is having faith that every single obstacle or problem in your way will be eliminated with the power of Jesus Christ and prayer. Freedom is knowing you have already won the war despite the difficult battles ahead. Freedom is a work in progress, and you cannot give up. God wants you to be successful beyond your wildest dreams. He literally placed the tools in the Bible and inserted resources into people to help all of us create a life we love. Do not let anyone ever tell you that you cannot find success across all fronts in business with God because I beg to differ. They are wrong.

With everything you have learned on this journey with me, I urge you to go fly. Fly higher and faster than you ever have before. Let the Holy, beautiful Spirit in you do what it does best, take you on a path to peace and prosperity.

And with my favorite quote of all time...

"But what if I fall.
Oh, but darling, what if you fly?"
By Erin Hanson

I wish you nothing but joy on your voyage. With God on your ship, there is not a chance yours could sink, Titanic icebergs and all (and yes Jack and Rose both could have fit on the door!) And if you ever get nervous in the car of life as you hit those curbs here and there, just ask Jesus to take the wheel.

Cheers, fellow entrepreneur! Cheers to you and your wildly successful business with God!

ACKNOWLEDGEMENTS

I want to thank my life partner, Taylor, for taking the time to listen to almost every chapter, even when you wanted to fall asleep most nights (and sometimes you did but that's okay ...as long as it was because you were tired and not bored.). Thank you to my dad who was ready for this book to be published as soon as I wrote the introduction. Special thank you to my mom who I know will tell every single person she knows and meets about this book.

Many thanks to my future-mom-in-law, Ms. Dumas-Cook, for helping me to remember to always keep God in the forefront despite the chaos. To Jackie, who let me read so many chapters to her over the phone and kept me encouraged even when things got hard. I will always appreciate those messages of asking me how far I was in typing this book.

Though you are not with me grandma, your entrepreneurship spirit burns in me like fire. This story could not happen without you. And your hubby, grandad, keeps reminding me that I can fly, and I just keep believing him.

Finally, a huge thank you to my friends and family who simply continue to enable me to keep doing the craziest things I can think of but somehow change lives while I am at it. You keep me on a path of wild, insane passion, yet I would not have it any other way.

Sabriya Dobbins, award-winning Founder of Project Passport and Life Discovery Expert, graduated from North Carolina State University with dual Bachelor's degrees in Animal Science and Social Work. Sabriya has a well-rounded background from working with disability adults to real estate sales, marketing, higher education, and various other fields. With skills gained from her combined career and volunteer experiences nationally and internationally, she launched Project Passport in 2019. Project Passport is a proactive wellness service company designed with the goal of providing preventative mental wellness tools and solutions to companies, organizations, and individual women. After experiencing severe anxiety and panic attacks, she realized there needed to be a sacred space to help people with the "little things" before they become big things that result in breakdowns. Sabriya is the author of the wellness blog *Living Life Full Force* and has certifications in Positive Psychology, Cognitive Behavioral Techniques Coaching, Neurolinguistics Practitioner-style Coaching, along with many other disciplines.

As a Master Life Coach and Master's in Clinical Mental Health Counseling Candidate at the University of the Cumberlands, she innovated a unique style of serving clients using experiential, actionable, and engaging mental wellness activities that are easy to duplicate and use outside of retreats or sessions. She applies her unique mental health skill base as a life coach and therapist intern where her clients move quickly to their goals and accomplish growth with a solution-focused perspective.

Sabriya believes in creating transformational experiences that help participants address their mental well-being in the present rather than escape their problems. In 2021, Sabriya was awarded the prestigious, international Sir Clyde Rivers Youth Empowerment award for her mental health service and two levels of Toastmasters International Speaking contests. After achieving success serving companies and women around the world in supporting their mental wellbeing through her work at Project Passport, she is focused on teaching others how to implement effective wellness and life skills programming in their individual lives and organizations. Sabriya has been featured in places like the NC State University Social Work Department, *AP UK*, *Authority Magazine*, *DataBird Business Journal*, *CEO Blognation*, and in many other publications.

She currently resides in St. Cloud, FL with her life partner, Taylor, and her sweet dogs, Zeus and Penelope. When they are not rocking at Disney, they are enjoying mother nature at all of the gorgeous Florida parks and recreation areas. You can learn more about her at: **sabriyadobbins.com**